AN AMERICAN IN KRAKOW
LIVING IN POLAND

CHRISTOPHER BLOSWICK

ISBN-13 978-1496181442
ISBN-10 1496181441

Contents

Introduction

I've lived here for a few years now, and my fellow Americans have asked me from time to time, "What's it like in Poland?" I've always wanted to tell them so much more than the occasion permitted. How do I sum up an entire country, an entire society? What do the people who live here consider to be important? What do I consider to be important? One day, upon the urging of my Polish wife, I started jotting down notes about the little peculiarities of life in Poland. Before long I realized I was well on my way to outlining a book on the subject.

I have Polish roots and see modern Poland as an extension of my heritage. Originally, I travelled to Poland thinking I would learn to speak a few Polish phrases, tour the historical sites, and see what the old country looked like today. I ended up falling for a remarkable Polish woman – a role model for a new generation of ambitious and successful career women in Poland – who would take my perspective on life here to a whole new level. The Poles are sometimes a little perplexed by this story, since when an American comes over and gets himself a Polish girl, that's usually her ticket out of the country. Just my luck – I found one who wanted to stay. I've since become part of a Polish family, overcome a plethora of bureaucratic hurdles, and settled down and built a house here. I thus continue to watch with great personal anticipation as Poland and Polish society progress.

Modern Poland is slightly larger in geographical area than the American state of Nevada, though farther north in latitude and covered in farmlands. Poland's natural landscape features scenic lakes, rolling mountain ranges, and lush, primal forests inhabited by rare examples of European bison. The country is divided into 16 "voivodeships" – but to make life easier for English readers I'll simply refer to these as provinces. I've travelled from one end of the country to the other, dipping my toes in chilly Baltic waters on the northerly beaches of Sopot, and hiking around in the Carpathian Mountains lining the southern border. I've wandered the cobblestone streets of antique town centers, stuffed myself with thousands of savory little *pierogi*, viewed Warsaw from on high atop the Palace of Culture and Science, and paid my respects at the marble-hewn tombs of Poland's kings and heroes in Wawel Castle.

Though reminders of Poland's communist past were everywhere in the form of architecture and infrastructure from those times, the gray blocks of standardized, communist era apartment buildings have been redressed in brighter colors, giving them a more contemporary feel better suited to the advancing Polish world. Meanwhile, flashy business districts and modern living spaces have risen amidst the older urban landscapes. Dated passenger trains still clunked along on aged railways across much of the country, but high speed rail was on its way together with the continued development of a modern highway network. Little-by-little following the initially rapid transformation from communism, Poland was still being reshaped.

Further diversifying Poland's eclectic style was the beautifully maintained architecture from the country's Renaissance and Baroque periods. Ornate, gilded palaces and churches informed the visitor of Poland's rich "golden age". The countryside too was dotted with the ruins of stone castles which long ago defended the once vast realm known as the Polish-Lithuanian Commonwealth. In some cities, an urban tram ride from the modern suburbs to the oldest central areas took one past nearly a thousand years of Polish architectural history.

To me, the Polish people have been gracious hosts and caring friends. Old stereotypes of Poles always failed to grasp the diversity and charm of the Polish people. Polish grandmothers certainly lived up to their reputation for never letting their guests go hungry. When exiting an elevator, Poles said goodbye to each other even if they were complete strangers who hadn't spoken a word beforehand. When an elderly lady boarded a crowded tram or bus, younger men and women were quick to surrender their seats to their senior. When a Polish man was introduced to a group of people, he would customarily greet the ladies first – sometimes even with an old fashioned kiss on the back of the hand.

As an American, it was easy for me to relate to Polish sentiments and aspirations. I found a familiar patriotic spirit, and an appreciation for the country's often difficult history was enshrined in memorials and monuments in practically every Polish city. The average Pole could still be a bit of a rebel below the surface, but the Poles' long struggle for national liberation has generally given way to more normal considerations like economic prosperity and upward mobility. Unfortunately, Polish politics had a very familiar feel to it as well, frequently characterized by dramatic theatrics and divisive partisanship which would have been quite at home in the United States Congress. As with their American counterparts, Poland's politicians could probably get a lot more done for their country if they spent less time quarreling amongst themselves.

Some Poles did enjoy a swig of vodka on occasion – often more than just a swig – often more than just on occasion. Polish people were eager for any excuse to celebrate, and it was almost impolite to refuse a drink at a social event without good reason. True enough, Poles sometimes had a habit of trying to do things in their own, unconventional ways. They were perhaps inherently inclined toward cleverness, coming from a culture which spent a couple of centuries learning to subvert and circumvent foreign administrations and communist authorities. Still today, some were constantly trying to bypass the rules to get away with perceived little victories against the society around them. Of course, pervasive bureaucracy and the occasional minor authorities all too eager to demonstrate their petty powers only perpetuated frustrated attitudes.

While Poland's roughly 38 million people represented a variety of social leanings, religious tradition was important in this largely Catholic country. Family dinners on Christmas Eve and crowded churches on Easter Sunday were predictable characteristics of Polish life even among those not particularly devout, and basically every Catholic holiday was an official day off from work. The Poles observed a plethora of religious customs like the public blessings of Easter baskets by the priests and much celebration surrounding a child's first communion. At least a part of the population was especially dedicated to the Catholic faith, linking it inextricably with their concept of the Polish identity and holding an almost medieval reverence toward the role of the church in society.

At the same time, the dance clubs were as crowded as the churches every weekend with free spirited young merrymakers out looking to have a good time. Social progressives had made significant inroads into Polish cultural and political thought. A large segment of the country's population was overtly religious, but there was also a sizeable demographic that was not – leading at times to very vocal arguments between these components of Polish society.

Polish people – like people anywhere else – spanned the spectrum, and sometimes Polish mentalities were not so easy to appreciate. Poles could be terribly impatient with each other, and strangely eager to prove someone else wrong. The otherwise gentlemanly demeanor of a lot of Polish men seemed to disappear behind the wheel of a car, with overly aggressive motorists contributing to a lot of accidents. I've watched as a semi tractor trailer tried to pull under a viaduct that wasn't tall enough to pass beneath, forcing it to halt and earning its driver angry honking from motorists stuck behind it. In the United States, those motorists would instinctively begin to back up and probably even step out of their cars to help direct the semi driver out of the situation. In Poland, however, the irritated motorists pulled up directly behind the semi as if to punish its driver for his mistake, but in doing so locking everyone into an inescapable traffic jam. It was something of a metaphor for Polish mentalities from time to time.

Along the way I would discover an endless supply of minor curiosities, like how people seemed to pass along from generation to generation the knowledge of which mushrooms in the forest were edible delicacies. Meteorologists on the news would officially report if the day's weather would have a positive or negative effect on *meteopatas* – people whose sense of well being was supposedly influenced predictably by the weather. They say Poland is a country full of hypochondriacs, and watching Polish television it was easy to see how people might get that impression. Every other TV commercial was for some kind of over-the-counter medication. One thing I did not find popular in Poland was Polka music, something often associated with the Polish-American community but actually of Czech origin. Of course, every Pole knows that the legendary half-French composer and pianist Fryderyk Chopin was Polish. What I didn't immediately realize was that "disco polo" – a sort of disco-pop-hip-hop looking like some kind of music video parody – was actually a popular genre of music among some Poles (though looked down upon by others).

The first decade of the 21st Century was a period of rapid growth for the country. When economic recession hit Western Europe toward the end of the decade, Poland famously remained the only national economy in the EU to see continued expansion. A lot of Poles were still relatively poor by Western European standards, but the economy had come a long way from the decades under central planning and many people were equally quite affluent. Suburban Poland sprawled with block after block of attractive private homes. The lack of parking everywhere made it seem like everyone owned a car – even if many were fifteen years old and bought secondhand in Germany.

As the first decade of the new century gave way to the next, economic growth was slowing with prolonged economic stagnation across Western Europe catching up to Poland. Unemployment was rising again, and much of the country's success in the preceding decade was attributed to the Poles' eager, post-communist embrace of consumerism, something that gradually moderated as uncertainty about the future grew. Housing prices and private household debts had risen quickly as Poland integrated itself into the European Union. Significant income inequality and discouraging youth unemployment remained serious concerns for Polish society, even as the overall economy continued to expand. The euro zone's various financial crises offered Poland's leadership important lessons to learn with respect to government debt levels and admittance to the common currency, though as time went by it appeared the country would be spared the worst of the continent's fiscal woes.

Occasionally upon telling Poles that I live in their country now, the response I've gotten has been that with so many people leaving Poland to work abroad or even emigrating permanently, it's good to see people actually coming the other way – moving *to* Poland. I feel a measure of satisfaction when I hear that, hoping I've offered some tiny reassurance to my Polish friends that in spite of present day challenges, the future they're building is one that's worth being a part of. Yes, trying to get things done in Poland can still be very frustrating at times. I would certainly be negligent in painting a purely positive image of life in Poland, but I've nevertheless found the things I like about living here to be worth the difficulties to date. I simply keep reminding myself that the upcoming generation of Poles has grown up in a Poland more exposed to and interconnected with the West than at any time in Poland's history. They've come to see how things work elsewhere, and won't long tolerate ineffective or outdated conditions and norms.

My Polish journey began with an interest in history and genealogy which encouraged me to learn more about the lands of my ancestors. Probably like most Americans interested in their Polish roots, I was initially inclined to look to the past, as the first few chapters of this book will attest; though actually living in Poland for some time I've gradually turned my attention to Poland's future. This is not a history text, but in describing my travels around Poland it is necessary to provide some background to create a fuller picture of the intrigue and inspiration I've found in this part of the world. The historical commentary is my interpretation of the wealth of information available at museum exhibits found throughout Poland, in addition to the writings of various authors listed at the end of this book whose works I highly recommend to anyone interested in the broader Polish story.

I grew up on an island called Mackinac on North America's vast Great Lakes, and worked as a mariner for a time before moving on to the world of business management. Perhaps it is in the blood of all islanders to look to the horizon and wonder about what lies beyond. For many years, something deep inside was telling me I needed to find my place in a story that started long before I was born. I'm an American now living in Poland, and this book is my insight into that land.

Chapter One
Why Poland – Family and History

A bit of background is necessary before going into detail about my experiences in Poland. Most Americans I know are not very familiar with Poland and might have difficulty understanding why one of their fellow citizens might chose to live there. To the average American, modern Poland is something of a blank spot, a mystery, a place which is difficult to categorize simply because it isn't a subject which comes up. Countries like England, Ireland, France, and Germany are more frequently referenced in American culture, and even then only superficially. The average American may be fairly certain that Warsaw is Poland's capital, the name Lech Walesa may be correctly associated with the end of communism, and Catholics may remember that Pope John Paul II came from Poland. But beyond that, America's familiarity with Poland is rather limited to a select few who have Polish ancestry or have made an above average effort to be knowledgeable about the world beyond their borders.

Where I came from in the wooded lake lands of Northern Michigan, most people with Polish roots were descended from 19th Century immigrants who'd long since lost most of their ethnic distinctiveness. A few might be able to say that a great-grandparent or an elderly aunt used to speak Polish, but the majority have become thoroughly Americanized. More recently, modern Polish migrants came and went with other Eastern Europeans following the collapse of the Soviet Union, taking seasonal work available in the local tourism industry. This usually meant cleaning hotel rooms or working in kitchens or similar positions. The practice tapered off, however, as migrant

Polish workers gained access to the labor markets of countries like the United Kingdom and Ireland when Poland joined the European Union in 2004.

During the mass migrations from Europe in the 19th Century, my Polish ancestors took what must have seemed like a one way journey to America. My rather English sounding surname "Bloswick" is somewhat misleading. Bloswick, in fact, was once the Polish name Błażejczyk. As the average American reader instantly concludes, this word is completely foreign and unpronounceable by the American tongue. It is spoken something like "bwah-zhey-chick" in the original Polish, but to an American it looks like I accidentally dropped something on the keyboard while I was typing.

Though in the United States today one can legally change one's name to Elvis, the Bloswick name change was accomplished for the sake of practicality. This was how my great-grandfather, Francis Błażejczyk, dealt with his difficult surname in the America of 1917. Ironically, the transformation of our Polish name from Błażejczyk to Bloswick happened just a year before the restoration of an independent Polish state in Europe as the Central Powers and Imperial Russia withdrew from the lands of old Poland.

My great-grandparents, Francis Blazejczyk and Mary Brzezinska, in a photo taken at their wedding in 1901

To begin with, I have to point out that I'm only a quarter Polish, and my paternal grandfather – the last to have both a Polish father and mother – didn't bother to pass on what little he knew of the Polish language to his sons. Sadly, it had lost its usefulness to him living in America. Grandpa John was the family's second generation to be born in the United States, and in those days people did everything they could to fit in. What did saying he was Polish do for him other than to make everyone immediately drag out their best "Polack jokes"? It didn't help that his Polish-American mother was apparently irritated by his marriage to a non-Pole and a non-Catholic – my Anglo-American grandmother.

People in Poland today might have found my grandfather a familiar personality though. According to my dad, whenever Grandpa John started out with, "Let's go have some fun, son," this meant hard labor was soon to follow. "Fun" meant shoveling coal, pulling used nails from old boards for reuse, or stripping the rubber insulation from discarded wiring to resell its copper core. Someone in Poland would later tell me, "In Poland, we don't throw anything away." It was a sentiment I think my grandfather would have appreciated.

Though my dad would occasionally make offhand remarks about us being Polish, my first active interest in Poland probably didn't start until university when I was participating in an international marketing class. I had to prepare a brief presentation on the business environment in a foreign country. It was then when I chose, I suppose out of some lingering sense of responsibility, to research post-communist Poland. I was subsequently impressed by Poland's successes in the rapid transformation out of the communist system, and curious about the changes in society that had taken place in recent years. From there, being a fan of history, I made the natural leap to reading about Poland's long and eventful past.

Parts of old Poland's history read like the

descriptions of a mythical kingdom from the Tolkien novels, with references to golden ages passed and alliances between the nations, wars with the barbarous armies of the east, scenes of lance-wielding cavalry charging across the battlefields, and the underlying theme of the rise and fall of a great realm which would one day rise again. Going back to where history gave way to legend, one could even find tales of dragons dwelling in the caves beneath the royal castle in Kraków.

Nevertheless, my high school history textbook basically ignored Poland until the country's first mention as the place the Nazis invaded in 1939, sparking World War Two. Such a general lack of information doubtless helped to facilitate negative stereotypes of Poles which have existed in America. I remember being surprised to learn that Poland was once the dominant power in Eastern Europe at a time when a nascent Russia was still a modest duchy around Moscow beholden to the marauding Mongols. Old Poland's political class drew upon the ancient Roman Republic for inspiration, and its academia produced such noted minds as the revolutionary astronomer Kopernik – known in English by his Latin name, Copernicus. The country reached its peak when it forged a united state with neighboring Lithuania for several centuries, encompassing a territory stretching from the Baltic Sea to the Black Sea larger than any other in Europe for a time. Personally, I saw noteworthy parallels between the former Polish-Lithuanian Commonwealth and the United States today – both in their merits and in their flaws.

Like the United States, the Polish-Lithuanian Commonwealth was a cosmopolitan, multiethnic realm. It was comprised of Poles, Lithuanians, Eastern Slavs, Germans, and Jews; but adopting the Polish language and even a Polish identity was then a mark of social status among the country's nobility, as Polish society carried Western ways eastward[1]. The noble class – the stratum of lords and knights – embraced a surprisingly democratic mentality for their era, ultimately making their king an elected monarch in 1573. *"Nic o nas bez nas"* meaning "nothing about us without us" was the nobility's motto toward the concept of government[2]. This sounded a lot like "governments… deriving their just powers from the consent of the governed" as the American Declaration of Independence would proclaim centuries later. Religious tolerance too was a key feature of Poland-Lithuania at a time when Western Europe was embroiled in religious wars between Protestants and Catholics[3]. Catholicism predominated in the Commonwealth, but Eastern Orthodoxy and Protestant faiths had significant followings, and Jews arrived en masse to escape persecution elsewhere in Europe.

The Commonwealth's days were numbered, however. Anger in Ukraine over increasingly exploitive Polish rule arose among the peasantry and Cossack militia. Armed rebellion soon followed, encouraging the westward expansion of a rising Russia amidst the instability. Along with cultural stagnation, the Commonwealth struggled under the high costs of successive wars, a factionalized political spectrum, and a disconnected class of ruling elites whose wealth and power contrasted starkly with the impoverished conditions of the masses. The May 3rd Constitution of 1791 was rejected by powerful aristocrats within the Commonwealth whose overriding privileges were threatened by reforms that might have preserved the deteriorating state. By 1795, the territory of a corrupt and chaotic Poland had been divided up by its neighbors – Imperial Russia, the Kingdom of Prussia, and Habsburg

Austria.[4]

To me, it was a fascinating and frankly pertinent story as the modern United States faced deep cultural and political divides, the undemocratic influence of the wealthiest financiers on American politics, and massive government debts mounting amidst costly wars. Poland's story didn't end in 1795, of course, and the Polish state was eventually restored as the Second Polish Republic at the end of the First World War. But more on all that later. It was the epic story of old Poland which encouraged me to dive further into my family's Polish roots. The collapse of this former European superpower quickly became a very personal thing to me, since my Polish ancestors had emigrated to America during Poland's arduous, 123-year absence from the map of Europe.

In the early 1800s, my Polish forefathers lived in the northwest of the former Polish-Lithuanian Commonwealth, the territory which had been claimed by Prussia (one of the German kingdoms) following old Poland's division. Most of my family's story was recounted by my Great-aunt Clara, the oldest surviving member of the Bloswick family. From what she told me, my ancestors were pretty typical examples of the Poles moving to America at that time. German policy generally promoted Polish emigration in those days, since it would gradually result in a smaller Polish population[5]. Great-great-grandpa Jan (John) Błażejczyk was a fur trader from Poznań. His wife Wiktoria (Victoria) was from a dressmaker's family. Great-great-grandpa Marcin (Martin) Brzeziński had to escape the old country to avoid being conscripted into the German army and forced to fight for the foreign regime then ruling his homeland. He would go on to marry the daughter of Polish migrants from the Kashubia region near the Baltic Sea, probably working class Poles or peasant folk who had arrived in America even earlier.

Despite my own diverse genealogy and very American upbringing, the more I learned about my Polish background and Polish history in general, the more I came to the conclusion that there was something special about Polish heritage, something enduring. Even after the generations spent in America, it was this latent sense of self-identification instilled in me unconsciously by my father which obliged me to choose Poland in that international marketing class. It drove me to explore my roots further and ultimately to be the first person in my family to set foot in Poland over 150 years after my earliest Polish ancestors left for America.

Perhaps ironically, the year I graduated from university my first visit to Europe was actually a few days spent on vacation in Germany. A cousin of mine was a NATO officer stationed there with the US Army, and he invited me for a stay with his family in the city of Heidelberg. I was certainly excited by the chance to explore any part of Europe and grateful for the opportunity. Of course, today's peaceful Federal Republic of Germany is far removed from its Prussian-dominated, 19th Century predecessor. These days Germany is Poland's biggest export market.

While genealogy and ethnography are obviously subjects I find interesting, this should not be confused with ethnic nationalism, something which has brought about much suffering in Europe even in recent history – though it admittedly played its role in preserving the Polish identity during times of foreign rule. Europe, thankfully, has made a lot of progress since my ancestors left for America. Driving through the ghostly remains of empty border crossing posts between European Union nations is an almost surreal experience. Given the unpleasant history between countries like Poland and Germany, the fact that a person can now cross unchecked from one to the other speaks volumes. One cannot understand modern Poland without also understanding the broader framework of the European Union, of which Poland is now an integral part.

Chapter Two
First Impressions – Old World Charm, Disco Clubs, and Strange Bathroom Symbols

By 2009 I was ready to embark upon my first journey to Poland. Americans could spend up to 90 days within the borders of the European Union without an EU visa, so all I needed was my passport and a suitcase. I enrolled in a 1-month language course at Kraków's historic Jagiellonian University – an educational facility established in 1364 by King Kazimierz the Great. I considered studying in Poznań where most of my Polish family had originated, but Kraków (pronounced "crack-oov" in Polish) was historically old Poland's first city and the traditional center of Polish education. Even under foreign rule during the 19th Century, Kraków remained the most open forum for the expression of Polish thought and culture. It made sense to me at the time, and I was encouraged by the professional appearance and all-inclusive nature of the university's Polish Language for Foreigners program.

It was at the international airport in Chicago while waiting for my flight that I first happened to meet Polish-Americans who, like me, still had some sense of attachment to the old country. They too were on their way to the summer language course in Kraków, sponsored by the Kosciuszko (kosh-choosh-koh) Foundation in the United States – a Polish-American cultural and educational organization. They were young, mostly college age and fresh out of high school, and I'd overheard them talking about the language school in Poland. We forged an immediate connection and would keep in touch for the duration of the program.

My fellow language students tended to be second generation Polish-Americans – the descendents of more recent immigrants to the United States. Many of them still had family in Poland. Their parents and grandparents had known Poland under the difficult years of Soviet-imposed communism. They had grown up hearing from their elders about a Poland of rationing, cueing, shortages, corruption, and the repression of political decent. It was a Poland I knew little about. My family had emigrated to America long before, in an era when the very idea of Poland was but a romantic memory of a lost kingdom. If I was still a Pole, I felt as if I was a Pole from another time.

On the 5th of July, 2009, I stepped off the plane onto Polish soil. I was thrilled. I remember an inexplicable sense of pride welling up inside me as soon as I saw the Polish flag flying over the airfield. The clean, modern feel of the Kraków airport was a reassuring welcome as I officially entered the country. Our little Polish-American group agreed to split a cab, and we were quickly off to our first destination – the student dormitory "Piast" named after old Poland's first ruling dynasty.

Our student dormitory (or *akademik* in Polish) was rather basic, an example of slightly updated, communist period institutional housing with surface wiring and piping, rudimentary furniture, no air conditioning, and some cracking concrete and plaster. Adjoining rooms shared a bathroom and a balcony. There were no fly screens on the windows, which I would quickly learn was typical in Poland despite the mosquitoes that come out in the evenings. If I recall correctly, I was on the 5th floor – which was the 4th floor by Polish reckoning. The ground floor was called the *parter* and what Americans called the 2nd floor was what the Poles called the 1st floor. Thankfully there was an elevator, but as was typical of communist era buildings, the elevator only had a door on the outside of the elevator shaft. The elevator cabin itself didn't have doors on the passenger side, thus it was advisable to step back from the entryway before the lift started to move. Though it all seemed a bit austere, a bit dated, the simple accommodations of the student dormitory were adequate for sleeping and studying, and I would soon find the cafeteria on the ground floor which served up thrice-daily samplings of hearty Polish cuisine.

Prior to the start of classes, several days elapsed which all sort of rolled together. I was too excited to be jetlagged, and I don't remember the exact order of things, or – for that matter – sleeping much. I remember taking some kind of placement test for my practically non-existent proficiency with the Polish language, and checking the information boards for a list of guided tours organized by the university. I attended orientation meetings and was introduced to our student advisors, English-speaking students from Poland who would live in the dorms with us and help us find our way around. They did a good job seeing that we found all the vital amenities, and they showed us how to get to our classrooms in nearby buildings. Much of the surrounding area was interspersed with university facilities and other student dormitories dating from the communist era or before. Fortunately for the Americans who typically had only a couple semesters of Spanish or French lessons behind us, the European students in our group had usually spent years learning the English language. New friends were made quickly, and getting together in the downstairs café to compare worldviews would become a popular afterhours diversion.

Street trams, antique architecture, and royal castles

Soon enough our young Polish student advisors were leading us to the tram stop nearest the dormitory to set off on our first official tour of Kraków. Along the city sidewalks, little kiosks, typically green in color, sold newspapers, magazines, cigarettes, beverages – and tickets for the public transportation system. However, the older ladies often working in these kiosks, though offering reassuring smiles, usually didn't speak English. A bit of pointing and nodding and other body language was required of foreign tourists making purchases, a language most European travelers quickly become quite fluent in. For non-Polish speakers, tickets could more easily be purchased from the multi-lingual vending machines found at some of the bus and tram stops. Not long after my first visit, they could also be purchased from dispensers installed directly onboard most public transports.

As soon as one boarded any mode of public transportation, it was necessary to find the little electric punches which stamped and validated one's ticket. Every now and then "controllers" would show up on the trams and walk from end to end checking that everyone had a validated ticket. A person caught riding without paying was issued a fine. Fortunately after arriving in the old town, most of the city's famous historic sites could be reached on foot.

The summer weather in Poland varies, but is generally warm. Cooler days are common in the early summer, while in late July and August it seems like there's always a week or two of very hot, humid weather. Earlier in the summer, one can easily be caught by intense, fast moving rain showers. More severe weather comes in the form of the *halny*, strong winds which can suddenly blow northward from Poland's southern mountains. Tornadoes are a rare occurrence, but together with the *halny*, powerful summer thunderstorms occasionally damage roofs and bring down trees. As much of Poland's landscape is made up of relatively flat plains, flooding is also a problem from time to time along parts of the country's rivers. Most of the time, however, summertime weather in Poland is moderate, sunny, and idyllic.

We took a crowded tram on a hot summer day from the urban sprawl west of the city center toward the historic old town. Instead of an underground metro system, above ground tramways crisscrossed the city on rails built into the streets and powered by a network of overhead electrical cables strung between the buildings. The twenty-minute ride took us past random shops and office structures, a growing number of modern apartment complexes, and lots of plainer housing blocks built during the communist era. As we neared the old city center, more antiquated façades began to appear.

A public tram running on the rails built into the city's downtown streets

Kraków is located in Poland's southerly province of Małopolskie (mah-woh-pol-ski-eh). The city became associated with Poland almost at the start of the country's official history, as Poland's founder, Mieszko I, extended his influence over the area through marriage to the Bohemian princess Dubravka. From 1038 to 1596, Kraków was Poland's capital, a fact which Kraków residents were quick to point out to foreigners whenever someone mentioned Warsaw. I would later come to realize there was a sort of rivalry between the two cities. Even following the transfer of government to Warsaw, royal coronations and funerals continued to take place in Kraków's royal castle until the end of the Polish monarchy, and Kraków today remains Poland's second largest city.

During the Partitions period of the 19th Century, the city lay within the borders of the Austro-Hungarian Empire, and much of Kraków's picturesque central architecture comes from this period. Among the plainer Polish modernist structures from the early 20th Century and the countless old gothic and baroque churches, one found streets lined with three, four, and five storey townhouses dressed in elegant, 19th Century façades. Their upper edges were decorated with sculpted cornices, and pediments and pilasters encompassed the windows and doors like the entrances to ancient Greco-Roman temples. The townhouses were usually built wall-to-wall with no passageways or alleys between them, but doorways from the sidewalks often opened to corridors which led through the ground floor toward central courtyards. Most of these buildings were filled with apartments in modern times, and some had storefronts and businesses at the street level.

The old town was but a tiny fraction of the modern city of Kraków, which had vastly expanded over the centuries. We entered old Kraków on foot through the Floriańska Gate. The passage led beneath the only remaining example of the high stone gate towers which once defended the town's perimeter. The street beyond leading to the main market square was lined with shops selling everything from Kraków-themed coffee mugs and t-shirts to expensive amber jewelry – for centuries a Polish specialization. The city's vast central plaza, surrounded by elegant townhouses, hotels, and storefronts, was the largest medieval town square in Europe. This was Kraków's living heart, the center of activity for tourists and locals alike – quite different from the more decentralized European destinations like Paris, London, and Berlin.

Crowds of tourists crisscrossed the plaza snapping

photographs, and packed full the outdoor restaurant patios lining the square's perimeter. The center of the market square was dominated by the long, renaissance-styled Cloth Hall (*Sukiennice*) with its arched colonnade and whimsical, curling pediments and spires. Merchants within once traded linens and spices from the Far East, while in modern times the Cloth Hall was filled with little booths hawking Polish folk crafts and knickknacks, and the museum in the rooms above displayed a collection of paintings and sculptures by Polish artists.

The east side of Krakow's main square, the Cloth Hall to the left and St. Mary's Basilica to the right

As I stood there on the market square beneath St. Mary's Basilica taking in all the sights and sounds, I was struck by the knowledge of the history this place had born witness to. The carriages of Poland's medieval kings had rolled past that very spot. On the opposite side of the square, the 18th Century revolutionary Kościuszko, after returning from fighting in the American Revolution, swore an oath to lead Poland's armed forces against the Partitioning Powers while simultaneously promising not to use his authority for oppression. Austrian soldiers marched across this plaza during the 19th Century. Their Nazi successors did the same thing during World War Two before abandoning the city to the advancing Soviet Army. Now Poles and Germans sipped tea together at the outdoor cafés, young couples met beneath the statues to start their first dates, and small children toddled around giggling as they chased the pigeons by the florists' tents.

It looked as though the old basement cellars and coal rooms beneath every second building in Kraków's old town had been converted into a bar, restaurant, or disco club. As the sun began to set, the downtown sidewalks bustled with sharply-dressed young men and women jaunting from club to club until the early morning hours. Some establishments were clearly marked and easy to find, while others were secreted away down long corridors and narrow steps. Neon lights accented the centuries-old brick walls inside, and an agglomeration of medieval and modern styles together with disco balls, lasers, and good acoustics created stimulating sensory environments.

The group of Polish-American students fresh out of high school must have been noting all the drinking establishments as we were touring the city center. They would take full advantage of the fact that Poland's legal drinking age was 18. For many, it was their first big trip away from home on their own, and in the States one could not purchase alcohol before 21 years of age. Before long, any day of the week it was easy to catch a group headed into the city center for a night on the town.

Coming from the United States, a melting pot of all the world's peoples, the conspicuous lack of ethnic diversity was inescapable when walking the streets of Polish cities. Even touring more westerly European cities like London, Paris, or Rome, one encountered large communities descended from Indians, Black Africans, or Arab North Africans in part owing to those European countries' long histories of overseas colonization. Poland, however, remained strikingly homogenous, with ethnic minorities a rare sight on city streets aside from occasional non-Caucasian tourists and students.

Poles came in all shapes and sizes, but Polish women were often exceedingly pretty. Most frequently they had slightly broad faces, sly Slavic eyes, pouty little smiles, and embraced a glamorous sense of style. Many of them looked like they must have worked at least part time as runway models. While blonde hair and black were pretty evenly distributed, red hair – or red hair coloring – was also common. Older women noticeably rarely let their hair go gray, often dying their curly locks in rather intense shades of red. Polish men could be on the stocky side with rounded faces and usually very short hair. Others were rather thin and a bit nerdy looking like myself, perhaps not surprising given Poland's reputation as a global destination for IT businesses. On occasion, one might see a Polish girl in heels and a short dress escorted down the street by a young Polish guy wearing jeans and a hoodie. A pseudo hip-hop style seemed to be fashionable among some teenage males, while older student types and career aged men dressed somewhat less casually than the average American, in line with slightly more stylish European trends. Elderly men could often be seen wearing flat caps or driving caps, something the American might expect to see worn by a golfer on the green.

A plethora of languages could be heard on the streets. While Kraków was a historic sightseeing destination for Poles from across the country, the city was also one of the best known Polish destinations for foreign tourists. Older German and Japanese tour groups seemed particularly common. American or Canadian accents were often heard – Kraków being a popular stop for North Americans of Polish descent. The French and Italians were frequent in pairs or families, and the Spanish came in sizeable troupes of varying ages. Though it took me a while to distinguish the audible differences from Polish, I would later begin to pick out occasional Eastern Slavic speakers as well.

Noticing the British usually took less effort. Wherever there was an unusually boisterous group swarming the tables at an outdoor café, it was made up of a bunch of young Englishmen downing pint after pint of inexpensive Polish beer. Kraków had its share of strip clubs, and groups of young Britishers typically came to Poland to have a rowdy bachelor's party at a more reasonable price than back home. To be fair, though, I've also observed that a group of young Polish men on holiday abroad was frequently the source of the loudest conversation in the room.

More mature British travelers were there too, but making a better effort to be discrete about it. They were the pleasant, older British couples spending their retirement years touring the sights all across Europe. I've heard more than one couple say that Kraków was quite possibly the most delightful continental destination they'd visited.

One unfortunate patron of the city streets was the

pigeon. They dwelled upon every high ledge dripping their droppings onto the sidewalks like messy painters who'd failed to lay down tarpaulins to catch their spills. Buildings everywhere were draped in fine nets and armored with strips of tiny little spikes on every horizontal ledge, yet still the pigeons prevailed. They roamed in herds across the market square, cooing in chorus, and were so numb to the presence of humans that a person could nearly trip over a pigeon before the ignorant little birds would move from one's path. There would be no eliminating this infestation, however. Legend held that the pigeons were once Polish knights turned into birds by an evil witch. Undeterred by their reduced status, they remained forever at their urban posts, watching over the city. The crafty little pigeons had gotten themselves enshrined in Kraków's legends, thus ensuring their continued presence.

The visitor to the city center didn't have to walk very far before finding an elderly lady manning a blue *obwarzanek* cart. The *obwarzanek* (ohb-vah-zhah-neck) was like a giant bagel with a similar thickness but crustier exterior than an American bagel, and not meant to be sliced open. These Kraków bagels came in a variety of flavors from salted to cheese covered, and every morning the little blue carts were filled to the brims and wheeled out to their sidewalk stations to tempt passing pedestrians. They didn't cost much and were quite filling, so they were popular with students who'd skipped breakfast on their way to class.

Departing the main market square via Grodzka Street took us past more townhouses, shops, cafés, and churches, and ultimately led us to Wawel (vah-vel) Castle. For almost 600 years, this fortified hilltop was the residence of Poland's kings. Over the centuries, successive regimes – drawn by the historical association of Wawel

Hill with power – had built new structures atop the old. Buried within the ancient mound were the ruins of past residences dating from before recorded times. Deeper below was a series of natural caves fabled to have been the dwelling place of the *Smok Wawelski*, the Dragon of Wawel. Legends claimed the beast terrorized the local villagers before being slain upon the order of Prince Krakus, the mythical founder of Kraków.

The green, grassy hill itself was ringed by a faceted wall of redbrick bastions. Above these bulwarks rose a collection of fortified towers and gothic cathedral spires capped with metal-plated, copper-green bell towers. Old paintings and photographs suggested the castle was once coated in plaster, but preservation work had left bare many of the complex's brick and stone walls. The royal residences, however, surrounding a large, colonnaded courtyard on the north side of the hill retained their sleek, renaissance appearance.

The renaissance castle buildings and gothic cathedral were pilgrimage points for the Polish people and for foreigners like me with Polish roots. The cathedral and its subterranean crypt held the tombs of most of Poland's kings, as well as national icons like General Kościuszko who fought for both Poland and the United States in the late 18ᵗʰ Century, Marshal Józef Piłsudski who led the Polish state in 1918 after the country regained its independence, and writers like Mickiewicz and Słowacki whose words helped to keep the Polish spirit and identity alive under foreign rule. More recently, Karol Wojtyła performed masses here as Archbishop of Kraków before becoming Pope John Paul II.

Wawel Castle in Krakow, the seat of Poland's kings from 1038 to 1596

Urban living and countryside vistas

Walking southeast from the old town, one arrived in Kraków's Kazimierz district, the realm of aspiring artists and vagabonds as well as the site of flea markets and outdoor vegetable stands. For centuries the area was home to a sizeable Jewish minority, a people once far more numerous in Poland. Most of the Polish Jews were killed during the genocidal Nazi occupation of World War Two, but by the early 21st Century a small and active Jewish community had reemerged here. The oldest synagogue in Poland, dating from the 15th Century, is located in Kazimierz, and several other historic Jewish temples and cemeteries can be found among Kazimierz district's maze of narrow streets.

Though naturally a draw for passing tourists, Kazimierz's many cafés and bars were also frequented by the locals and students. The café lifestyle was a part of the European experience which I quickly came to appreciate in Kraków. Sitting at an outdoor table and watching the steady stream of leisurely foot traffic made the city feel alive and human. In the United States, one typically ate at an indoor restaurant when going for a meal in the city. We Americans are very inclined toward our climate controlled environments, running from our air-conditioned cars into air-conditioned buildings. There are exceptions, but our urban cores tend to be much larger and more decentralized, often lacking a walkable center where everyone goes to soak up the atmosphere. Strolling with the crowd, window shopping, and watching passersby from a table are habits more likely to be found in large, indoor shopping malls in the States.

Outdoor cafes lining the streets and plazas of Krakow's Kazimierz district

Generally, Kraków's residents looked to be pretty active. The city had a rather young demographic, hosting plenty of universities and academies filled with often health conscious students – though others smoked like chimneys and drank like sailors. Recreational exercise was a common sight, and swimming pools and gyms were crowded. While bicycle lanes were intermittent and pedestrians had a habit of ignoring them, plenty of people still peddled around, taking advantage of the city's relatively flat central landscape. Conveniently, bicycles were allowed on the streets as well, though similarly operating at their own risk (more on Polish drivers in Chapter Five). A broad, paved pathway stretched for kilometers along the Vistula River, and the section passing by the royal castle and Kazimierz district was constantly abuzz with cyclists, joggers, and walkers. Along this busy route, people also lounged on the grassy embankments above the river, often stripping down to their swimsuits and soaking up the sun on brighter days. This was Catholic Poland, however, and not the French Riviera, so you probably won't see any topless sunbathers. Though a few Polish girls who came unprepared occasionally appeared in their bras rather than swimsuit tops.

In the old town center, the renaissance and baroque styled buildings were maintained like works of architectural art, but there were also many buildings beyond the city center which, for various reasons, were in very poor condition. Numerous townhouses here and there remained in an unfortunate state of disrepair. Aside from sad instances of vandalism by spray-paint-wielding hooligans, a common problem was the issue of ownership rights which plagued many older properties after the transition from communism. A meticulous legal system saw disputes lasting in some cases for decades.

Moreover, during the communist takeover following World War Two, the authorities seized control of privately-owned residence buildings and divided large apartments into smaller ones. The bourgeois property owners apparently had too much room to themselves, so more families were moved in to share the sub-divided accommodations. After the communist system was overturned, property ownership usually returned to the original owners or their descendents, but people who had become residents during the communist years had to be given the option to continue residing in the formerly public housing at a very low rate of rent. As a result, some downtown buildings fell into disrepair because the owners couldn't charge adequate rent to cover the maintenance bills. The cost of restoring the exteriors of the old townhouses could easily be prohibitive as many buildings required expensive, specialized work to preserve their historical character.

Heavily soot-stained buildings were a common sight. High levels of pollution were a problem in Kraków, with lots of traffic allowed to flow through historic downtown areas as well as the burning of coal in unfiltered household stoves for winter heating. Kraków lies in a basin surrounded by hills and low mountains, so dirty air often rests stagnantly atop the city. Pollution levels left exterior walls caked in black if not routinely cleaned.

Poland possessed abundant coal reserves making this a very affordable, though very dirty, domestic fuel source. The construction of nuclear power plants was an expensive prospect, and at times Poland was paying more for natural gas from Russia than wealthier EU states farther west[6]. A liquefied natural gas terminal on the Baltic coast was in the works in order to import gas from other suppliers, and studies were in progress looking to tap Poland's potentially vast shale gas reserves through the controversial "fracking" method – if only Poland's bureaucratic governmental apparatus could avoid scaring away companies possessing the necessary technical expertise[7]. However, until these options or reliable renewable sources produced tangible alternatives, coal would continue to dominate in Poland's energy mix. At the least, Poland's reliance on its own coal resources make the country significantly more energy independent than other EU states, needing to import a little over 30% of its energy compared to the EU average of over 50%[8]. That is, until the Poles run out of coal.

Beyond Kraków's center with its charming renaissance buildings and stylish, 19th Century architecture, much of the city, as with everywhere in Poland, expanded into rather plain, utilitarian structures built during the communist years as urban populations exploded. Contrarily, early communist period design – "socialist realist" architecture – was meant to inspire, to be a source of communal pride for working class residents. Wide avenues and sophisticated façades could be found in parts of Kraków's Nowa Huta district, a carefully planned, urban residential area intended for the newly elevated proletariat of the Stalinist period.

The socialist realist style soon gave way to practicality, and less inspired structures became the norm. Boxy, standardized apartment buildings built from prefabricated concrete panels stretched on block after block. Preformed concrete telephone poles augmented endless kilometers of sidewalks paved with concrete tiles which have settled unevenly over time, cracking and dissolving into gravel. Casual neglect, the steady deposition of soot, and a ready supply of graffiti left parts of the city looking a bit austere even in modern times. Fortunately, most of the communist period buildings have been remodeled over the past couple decades, resurfaced and painted to give them a brighter, more pleasant appearance. Such efforts, together with a boom in the construction of new buildings in Kraków, had made some improvements to Poland's communist era infrastructural legacy.

People continued to renovate the interiors of many of the old apartment blocks. During my later period in Poland, it was interesting to see how residents had customized these small, standardized units once the end of communism afforded people more diverse furnishing options. Walking from one apartment to the next, each had an equivalent layout and size, yet some were completely modern while others looked just as they did originally, right down to the old shelving units called *meblościanki* lining the longest wall in the room.

At some point, the communist planners must have decided that every apartment should have a balcony. Apparently they thought that every working class man should enjoy stepping out for a breath of the fresh air wafting in from all the heavy industry, and to be reminded that everyone else lived in the same sort of standardized housing towers. At any rate, the balconies gave people a place to have a cigarette and to hang their laundry in the warmer months. As space was at a premium in the little apartments, the balconies also ended up in use for the storage of bulky, weather resistant items like bicycles or foldable chairs for visiting guests.

As Poles have been kind enough to invite me into their homes over the years, probably the most interesting trend I've noticed was a recurring décor consisting of exotic artifacts accumulated on trips to far away countries. Some collected curiosities like tribal masks from Sub-Saharan Africa, musical instruments from the Aborigines of Australia, or the statuettes of Ancient Egyptian deities. There was almost always a crucifix near the front door of a Polish household, a reminder of Poland's longstanding Catholic tradition even among those not especially devout. One might also notice a peculiar little wooden figurine carved and painted in the form of a very stereotypical looking Jew, dressed in a black coat and hat, with a long beard and a big nose. As the superstition goes, supposedly having a little figure of a Jew on display in the living room of one's house would bring financial success. When visiting someone's home, Poles typically took off their shoes upon entering, or at least made a good show of asking if they should do so while automatically beginning to untie their shoelaces. With wood floors or linoleum common throughout Polish homes, a guest arriving at a Polish household might even be offered a pair of slippers at the door.

Not everyone lived in the big apartment blocks. People did build private houses even during the communist years, though it wasn't easy to accomplish. Back then, building materials for private projects could be difficult to come by. From what I understood, at times a lot of vodka had to change hands to siphon adequate bricks and cement from various public building sites or to have materials surreptitiously set aside by construction suppliers. Houses often sported a partially finished look for years as people gradually assembled the necessary materials. After the transformation to the market economy, the pace of construction accelerated and suburban areas have naturally been expanding. Nevertheless, it's still a common sight to see houses in varying stages of completion for a long time, since building a home is a complicated and expensive task often handled by determined individuals who do much of the finishing work themselves.

With the notable exception of the mountain areas, Poles usually built their homes from brick rather than wood as we do in the United States. My Polish wife would later describe the typical American home as an attractive but drafty box made from toothpicks. Polish houses had a very solid feel to them in comparison. Tiled or wood paneled floors were more common than the linoleum and carpet usually found in American homes, and even garages were often tiled as opposed to being left with bare concrete floors. The exterior walls of the Polish home were wrapped in hard Styrofoam insulation and coated with plaster. The roofs were usually covered in ceramic tiles of varying colors, but asphalt shingles like those common in the States could also be seen.

Where Americans were inclined to maintain neatly tended yards of grass on display for all to see, Polish people were avid secret gardeners. Suburban homes might be ringed by tall fences and walls of vegetation offering one's yard greater privacy. Behind their high fences, one might find blossoming oases, little stone walkways set into the grass, and relaxing outdoor patios among the gardens just a few steps in from any suburban Polish street.

Housing in Poland ranging from refinished, communist era apartment blocks to modern suburban homes

For Poles who didn't have private yards, the communist era tradition of the *działka* (jow-kah) continued, at least in places. The authorities under the old system set aside land here and there around the outskirts of Polish cities where they granted people allotments to be used for private cultivation. Narrow pathways ran like streets between row after row of little fenced off gardens. Tending these gardens gave urban residents something to do in their free time, and vegetables grown there for personal consumption added a bit more fresh produce to their diets. People often built rudimentary shacks on their plots to store their tools in or for use as private getaway cabins whenever they needed a break from life in the concrete towers. Even in modern Poland, going to the *działka* was a rather passionate hobby for some, particular elderly Poles.

When communism ended, Poland went through a rapid transformation to replace central economic planning with the decentralized, market-based economic structures of the West – the so-called "shock therapy" laid out by economist Leszek Balcerowicz. State run industries were privatized and foreign capital poured into the country, stimulating rapid economic growth[9]. It wasn't an easy transformation though, leading to the end of many inefficient businesses which, operating within the economically sheltered world of the former Communist Bloc, had served as centers of employment subsidized by the rest of society. The closure of uncompetitive operations left the country struggling with high unemployment. Though the situation began to improve in the years following Poland's 2004 accession to the European Union, the country continued to see unemployment above 10% at the start of the next decade[10].

Over 60% of modern Poland's economy was services-based, in contrast with the heavy industry favored by the communist planners[11]. Outsourced business services in areas like banking and finance have become one of the largest employers in Poland, taking advantage of the country's educated workforce and relatively modest wages[12] . Poland was also becoming a major European manufacturer as companies relocated production to Poland – at times controversially – from other EU states and elsewhere[13]. This was often pretty obviously aimed at taking advantage of the country's low wage levels (while corporate profits and tax revenues fled the country). But on the positive side, aside from jobs, knowledge and experience came along with such developments, advancing Poland's domestic business environment in the process. Coming from a management background myself, I would certainly emphasize the importance of cultivating a management culture on par with global standards when considering the long term health of the country's economy.

Kraków itself was a center for information technology and other knowledge-intensive enterprises, hosting offices for companies like Google, IBM, Motorola, Delphi, General Electric, and Comarch. The abundance of small businesses was also encouraging. Tailors and cobblers and other craftsmen could still be found along the city's streets, trades which have generally disappeared in typical American towns having unfortunately given way to cheaply manufactured, disposable consumer products. While several large hypermarket chains were dominant forces, there were still little bakeries and corner grocery stores and small retailers everywhere – even if many had become franchises themselves. Elderly Poles in particular benefited from the smaller shops located within walking distance of any group of apartment blocks. Already though, the Poles were being drawn from the difficult parking situations at downtown businesses to the convenience of having everything clustered together in giant shopping malls.

While the post-communist transformation certainly had the overall economy functioning more like those of Poland's wealthy western neighbors, it was obvious that many Poles were still comparatively poor. Generally individual income levels were rising, but remained well below the EU average[14]. Income varied by location, with more industrialized regions in the west of Poland and larger cities seeing faster growth than in rural or more easterly areas farther from EU export markets. At the same time, a lot of people in the cities too looked like working class folks living in tiny apartments and getting by on pretty limited salaries.

When considering income inequality in Poland, perhaps a relevant statistic was the country's level of union membership – particularly since Poland's break with communism began with an attempt to legalize independent trade unions. When the economy of the United States entered an important period of growth in the mid 20th Century, one factor contributing to narrowing income inequality and the rise of the middle class was Americans' growing participation in organized labor during those decades, peaking at around one out of every three workers[15] . In contrast, during the decade of economic expansion in Poland preceding my first visit to the country, the unionized percentage of the Polish labor force saw an overall decline, from more than 20% in 1999 to about 15% in 2009[16]. True enough, greater union membership and higher wages might have worsened the unemployment situation, and discouraged some of those foreign investors from relocating production to Poland. But the counter argument to that would be the fact that the average Pole is a pretty eager consumer, and if more Poles had more money in their pockets they would probably spend it, driving yet more economy activity. This is purely my own speculation, of course.

There were other considerations affecting the gains ordinary Poles have seen from their country's economic growth. Much of Poland was covered in farmland, and agriculture employed over 10% of the Polish workforce even into the second decade of the 21st Century (compared to less than 1% of the workforce in the United States)[17]. There were plenty of larger farms making use of modern mechanization, but then there were also the little Polish family farmers who could still be seen tilling their fields with dated equipment while their chickens scampered around in the yard and their milk cow wandered back and forth beside the road.

My Polish language course included trips outside Kraków along narrow roads crossing stretches of the countryside. Though we saw things only through the bubble of an air-conditioned motor coach on those trips, I would later come to learn it was a simpler world where traditional mindsets usually prevailed and the local priest was often at the center of the community. The rural scenery was pretty familiar to me as my mother's parents were farmers from the agricultural heartlands of my home state of Michigan, but the standards in Poland were more old-fashioned at times.

That characteristically tenacious spirit of the Polish peasant, which resisted Soviet-style collectivization and survived the quotas and price fixing of the communist period, insured there were a lot of smaller farms functioning even today. On the other hand, the ranks of the Polish agricultural worker have nearly halved in recent years. The smaller farmers may have finally met their match, coming under pressure to compete for subsidies with larger, more efficient farming operations in the face of a litany of new bureaucratic rules and regulations handed down by the European Union. Perhaps if modern society has a growing appreciation for organically cultivated food products and a greater dedication to preserving natural biodiversity, some traditional Polish farmers may still be able to earn a living.[18]

The rural Polish countryside north of Krakow

Outside the city there were also nice new houses going up everywhere, complete with pricey BMWs or Volkswagens parked in the driveways. Some homes belonged to Poles who worked in Kraków or nearby cities and sought a quieter private life beyond the suburbs. Other fanciful houses were built by Poles who'd perhaps worked abroad and returned to Poland with money enough to set themselves apart from their poorer neighbors. This they did by building very large dwellings, often adding decorative features like multi-storey columns or grand, arched entryways. It could all end up looking a bit tacky at times, but I've been told that owning a big manor house in the countryside reminiscent of those of the old Polish nobility – or the opulent country estates portrayed in American soap operas in the 1980s – was the dream for some.

Hearty Polish food

As the generations passed in the United States, my family lost any Polish culinary traditions they may have had. During that first month in Kraków I very quickly grew to enjoy a number of characteristically Polish dishes. Polish cuisine tended to be simple and hearty – the types of food one would expect to develop in a less than affluent countryside during cold, Eastern European winters. It was heavy on flour, potatoes, and cream, but it had many noteworthy tastes.

As I pointed out, Poland has an extensive and often very traditional agricultural sector. Thus the food in Poland is less likely to be genetically modified and more likely to emphasize natural ingredients. The Poles generally use real sugar as a sweetener instead of high fructose corn syrup. Fresh fruits and vegetables can actually seem to be more flavorful than what we've come to expect in the States. More than once I've heard Europeans complain that American cheese basically tastes like wax – and I'm not just referring to the French. Poles do their shopping mostly in supermarkets and bakery chains, but a few regular farmers' markets located around Kraków were routinely bustling. Polish people could often tell you what produce was in season and the freshest at any given time – spinach and asparagus in May, strawberries in June, tomatoes in

July, grapes in August and September – something Americans almost never consider as they walk into the perpetually standardized grocery section at Wal-Mart. Definitely a local specialization is honey, and since moving here I try to buy only Polish honey – a conscious consumer philosophy worth applying to a lot of agricultural products in Poland.

Perhaps the most recognizable Polish dish was *pierogi* – stuffed dumplings in a variety of styles. These could be filled with minced meat, potatoes and cheese, mushrooms, cabbage, or even fruits. One of my favorite courses was *żurek*, a sour rye soup typically filled with potatoes, sausages, and hardboiled eggs. Another favorite of mine was fried potato pancakes covered in goulash. A wide variety of sausages fell under the Polish word *kiełbasa*, and for those interested in cabbage – which personally I was not – there were plenty of options including *gołąbki*, traditional cabbage rolls stuffed with meat and rice, usually accompanied by a tomato sauce. Polish people also make a particularly sour and salty pickle, the *kiszony ogórek* (kee-show-nih oh-goo-rek), which can rarely be found in supermarkets even in Poland. They're instead a delicacy made at home to a variety of personal recipes. While pork products were an agreeable part of the Polish diet, I wasn't particularly impressed by the local beef. Better cuts were available for a higher price, but I got the impression ordinary Polish beef came on the market whenever someone's old milk cow keeled over.

*Pierogi, a traditional Polish dish of stuffed
dumplings dripping with melted butter*

Kompot was a classic Polish fruit beverage
comprised of mixed fruits cooked in water. Actually,
kompot was more often a crushed fruit stew than a
beverage, but it was worth trying for sake of tradition.
During the communist era this cheap but uncommonly
flavorful beverage apparently abounded, though I think it
has since seen declining popularity.

I have come across some particularly unusual items
in the Polish diet which I try to avoid – though not always
successfully. I joke occasionally with Poles that they use
components of animals which in the States we would
generally consider to be, shall we say, leftover parts. Cow
intestines, tongue, and chicken stomachs can be found in
supermarkets and on some restaurant menus. The chicken

stomachs were very tender and tasted, frankly, like chicken. But I just couldn't get past the knowledge that I was eating chicken guts. Cow tongue, if not completely skinned, will lick you right back as it slides around in your mouth. While I've heard of such things being eaten in the rural hills of Tennessee, their consumption was not widespread in the United States. To be honest, they weren't that popular in Poland either.

Steak Tatar (*Tatar wołowy*) could also be found on some menus. Its place in the Polish diet supposedly originated from Poland's small community of Turkic Tatars in the old Polish-Lithuanian Commonwealth. At a time when my Polish was still quite basic, I ordered what I thought was some kind of beef steak and was surprised to be delivered a pile of uncooked minced meat topped with a raw egg. I gathered this delicacy was generally safe if ordered at a decent quality restaurant. But in the United States, the serving of raw meat or egg was discouraged due to the risk of bacteria growth in uncooked meat and poultry. The real shame was that it was a high quality ground beef that would have grilled into a great hamburger. Ever since then, I've been careful to check the menu for the word "Tatar" when ordering a steak. As with the tongues and stomachs, raw beef was just a bit much for my weak American constitution.

One of the most common Polish meals was cold cuts together with the necessary components to build a sandwich. Cheeses, sliced tomatoes, cucumbers or pickles, and horseradish typically accompanied a variety of traditional breads. The Polish sandwich, however, was assembled atop a single slice of bread like a pizza rather than between two slices as in the United States. At a later occasion when having lunch with my Polish wife's family members, they seemed to chuckle at me a bit when I put a second slice of bread atop my sandwich. We later concluded they must have been thinking I was planning to take it somewhere, since a sandwich made between two slices of bread was usually an item to be carried away to work or a picnic.

Naturally, a wide variety of other foods were available, both traditionally Polish and international in origin. I've read that pasta was increasingly replacing the ubiquitous potato, and young people seemed to flock to McDonald's and KFC whenever they had a little money in their pockets. Ethnic cooking was the theme of many restaurants, so one could easily find Italian, Chinese, or Mexican options. In Kraków there were even classic American burger joints or exotic Georgian kitchens to choose from. As with elsewhere in Europe, there were plenty of Middle-Eastern *kebab* (*döner*) windows too, which served up spicy meat and vegetable wraps. But be sure to grab a handful of napkins before starting into this often messy meal. Many Polish restaurants stuffed their stacks of napkins into U-shaped holders after first spreading them into a fan and then folding them in half. These decorative stacks looked pretty on the table, but extracting the single loose napkin at the center of the fold was often a time consuming and embarrassingly clumsy process.

After subjecting one's stomach to steak Tatar or *kebab*, it might be advisable to flush a little bacteria killing alcohol through the system. The Polish beverage industry was far from limited to the distillation of vodka. While Poland produced various internationally renowned vodka brands like Sobieski and Belvedere, Poland also had a large brewing industry and produced a variety of other specialties. There were the bigger beer brands like Żywiec, Tyskie, Okocim, and Lech, and there were numerous smaller breweries and micro-breweries like Kraków's C.K. Browar located practically in the city center in an underground pub. A warning to the average American though, the standard Polish beer had a higher alcohol content than in the United States, and the typical glass size was a half-liter unless a customer specifically asked for a small beer.

After a nice dinner, one might be offered a *nalewka* (nah-lev-kah), a shot of a sweet liquor like Wiśniówka from cherries. One calls out "*na zdrowie*" (nah zdroh-vee-eh) when offering a toast, the Polish equivalent of "cheers" but meaning essentially "to health". Mead (*miód pitny* in Polish) was a traditional specialty as well, though not as commonly known to the average Pole. Mead comes from the fermentation of honey, and could be dangerously sweet in Poland.

A language invented on a cold day?

During the four weeks I spent in Poland on that trip, my classmates and I attended daily lessons in the Polish language which took up most of our morning hours. Our Polish textbook was written in English, but the classroom lessons were conducted entirely in Polish – with a lot of illustrations and hand gestures necessary in order to communicate. Polish is a Slavic language like Russian, though the two are far from interchangeable. With a lot of "r" and "v" and "z" sounds, it can sound like Russian at times to the average American, though I would describe Polish as more full-bodied. To the native English speaker, even ordinary Polish words can sound rather coarse at times like "*cześć*" (cheshch), "*rzeczywiście*" (zheh-chih-veesh-cheh), and "*brzmieć*" (bzh-mee-ech) – in English meaning respectively "hi", "indeed", and the verb "to sound like". Polish words are often pronounced with the teeth nearly clenched and the sounds shaped at the tips of one's scrunched lips. For a foreigner learning Polish, proper pronunciation can be aided by practicing outdoors on a frigid winter day, shivering in the cold, which I think may be how the language was originally invented.

Standard Polish is taught throughout the country, so a person from the northerly city of Gdańsk can easily communicate with someone from the southern village of Zakopane. Some minor regional differences in vocabulary do exist, stemming in part from the period when Poland was partitioned by foreign countries. More vocabulary of German origin can be found in western and southern areas than in central and eastern provinces. Poles from eastern parts of the country can sometimes be identified by the slight melody detectable in their speech – the way the intonation of their sentences rises and falls in successive waves. Living in Kraków, I've come to speak with a few "southerly" or "Galician" Polish characteristics including pronouncing the number three (*trzy*) more like "chih" instead of the standard "tzhih", and saying "on the field" (*na pole*) instead of "on the manor" (*na dwór*) to describe going outside.

A couple of more distinct, local dialects can be found which aren't necessarily intelligible to other Poles. These are centered in the southwesterly province of Silesia and among the Kashubian minority of the coastal province of Pomorskie. However, populations are mixed in these areas, and speakers of the Silesian and Kashubian dialects usually speak standard Polish with Poles from other parts of the country – sometimes with a heavy accent.

Visually, the Polish alphabet is only a slight variation on the Latin alphabet, so it's not as alien as Russian or Ukrainian. Polish contains a few modified letters like "ę", "ą", "ł", and multiple options for the letter "z". The pronunciation rules are also rather different from English. The "w" in Polish makes the "v" sound, for example. Thus Kraków is pronounced "crack-oov". The Poles roll the letter "r" like the Spanish, and love to combine as many consonants in a row as possible. Words like Szczebrzeszyn (the name of a city) or *chrząszcz* (beetle) might look unpronounceable at first, but are not as bad as they seem once you know the rules. That's not to suggest Polish pronunciation is easy though. There are plenty of tongue twisters which even the Poles sometimes struggle to speak.

Szczebrzeszyn, a small town in Poland known for confounding foreigners trying to say its name (shcheb-zheh-shin)

Some things might seem more convenient with Polish, like the lack of definite articles. Definite articles like "a" and "the" don't exist in Polish, so instead of saying "I see a cat" or "I see the cat", one simply says "I see cat". It's the grammar that's tricky, constantly changing the ends of nouns and adjectives depending on what role the word has in the sentence. Polish nouns have multiple genders too – masculine, feminine, and neuter – usually depending on the last letter of the word. "*Młotek*" (a hammer) is masculine, "*miska*" (a bowl) is feminine, and "*okno*" (a window) is neutral. Sure enough, with each different grammatical case, all three genders change their endings in different ways. While Poles make these changes to word endings in the course of their speech without thinking about it, the English speaker finds it necessary at the beginning to construct each Polish sentence like a mathematical formula.

Polish vocabulary is usually quite different from English, but a few Polish words have worked their way into the English dictionary like "kielbasa" for Polish sausage and "vodka" which literally means "little water" in Polish. Naturally, the Russians also lay claim to the origins of that last one. "Polack" in English comes from the Polish word "*Polak*", which simply means a Polish man, but in English the word was unfortunately adopted as an ethnic slur.

Polish has adopted many words which the English speaker could easily recognize like "*bar*", "*biznes*", "*hamburger*", "*komputer*", and a number of profanities. A Pole might seamlessly insert the words "*native speaker*" into the middle of a Polish sentence about someone's language skills simply because the Polish equivalent would take longer to say. Many words in Polish have a Latin, French, or German origin just as in English, so words like *"alkohol"*, *"dokument"*, *"kapitalizm"*, *"organizm"*, *"repertuar"*, *"traktor"*, and *"toaleta"* are pretty intuitive to the average English speaker.

The vast majority of the vocabulary, however, is Slavic in origin, which is far removed from English. For me, it took a long time to get Polish words to stick in my head. The sounds were so foreign and the words all blended together. I couldn't tell where one word stopped and the next began. It didn't help my assimilation of the language that many Poles who I met, particularly younger people, were eager to practice their English with me instead of speaking Polish. Though I suppose I'm not really complaining about that.

Showering with no curtains, money matters, and personal safety

Since this chapter of the book is something of an introductory look at modern Poland, there are probably a few more things I should add for the foreign traveler intending to visit the country. For me, Poland was far from an exotic destination and I really didn't experience any great sense of culture shock. Coming from Northern Michigan, the sight of a few Roma (Gypsies) begging on the sidewalks was something new, but in general this was a modern, westernized, European country. Europeans I know were far more surprised at the sight of large numbers of homeless people sleeping on the streets in big American cities. Of course, there were plenty of minor differences between the way things worked in the United States and in Poland. For example, the widespread use of sidewalks as parking spaces for automobiles took some getting used to.

One vital detail the average American needed to be aware of at the start was the higher voltage level in

Europe. The first thing the arriving American wanted to do was plug in his computer and send reassuring messages to worried family members who had never left the country before. A European electrical outlet produced a shocking 230 volts instead of the North American 120 volt standard. Most chargers for electronics like cell phones and laptop computers were labeled for both voltage levels, but it was important to check so as not to melt the wiring. Moreover, European electrical plugs had a pair of round connection pins rather than the blade-like contacts used in North America, so attaching an adaptor to the end of an American plug was necessary to deal with the different connection shapes.

Walking into the wrong bathroom was a danger for foreigners not familiar with the old Polish bathroom symbols. Public bathrooms in older buildings didn't always have the male and female figures typically affixed to the doors to denote which was the men's and which was the women's toilet. Instead, a triangular symbol on the door indicated the men's room and a circular symbol the women's. And on the subject of bathrooms, many showers in Poland consisted of a bathtub with no shower curtain. In Poland, one sat in the tub to shower instead of standing. Foreign guests in Polish households thus had a tendency to soak bathroom floors with overspray from showering while standing in the tub.

Since that first visit to Poland, one pleasant relief (pardon the pun) has been the gradual disappearance of pay toilets in private businesses in Poland – though they can certainly still be found. All around Europe, travelers needing relief would likely find only pay toilets available to them after leaving the airport or their hotel room. Apparently, only to the average American with a societal penchant for road trips and a common standard of hospitality spanning a continent did the concept of paying to pee seem peculiar, if not downright rude. Having to pay to use the restroom at a restaurant or a gas station went against our every instinct as potential customers. In Kraków, even at McDonald's I had to remember to keep my receipt to show the old lady guarding the toilets that I had purchased something. Otherwise it cost 2 *złoty* (zwoh-tih, the Polish currency).

Cleaning ladies didn't hesitate to walk into the men's restrooms to swab the floors while the toilets and urinals were still occupied by male patrons – a bit of a surprise the first time. Usually said cleaning ladies were middle aged to elderly, but from time to time they included rather attractive young women, which suddenly made my business at the urinal feel a little inappropriate. I was also surprised at some places to see a team of elderly toilet attendants waiting to rush into the restroom after I finished so they could check that everything was in order. Generally though, this meant that such restrooms were kept pretty clean.

And on the subject of McDonald's and other restaurant establishments, another difference from the business practices in the States was that free refills of drinks were not offered. In the States, ordering a beverage generally included at least one complimentary refill of a customer's glass or cup. In Poland, however, even the fast food restaurants often didn't allow customers to refill their drinks without purchasing new ones. Water was almost automatically set on the table at most dine-in restaurants in the States, while asking for a water at a restaurant in Poland meant paying for a bottle of water which would be impractically small and probably more expensive than a large beer.

"*Ma Pan drobne?*" This common phrase asking for

exact change was one quaint, but sometimes frustrating, cultural norm I encountered right away. Whether in a small shop buying souvenirs or at a big Polish branch of the French hypermarket chain Carrefour, I was constantly being asked for exact change. The sales clerks preferred to keep a long line of resigned customers waiting while I counted out exactly seventy-three *groszy* (groh-shih, Polish cents) from the disorganized collection of coins in my pockets. The disappointed stares from cashiers as I stood there with my 50 *złoty* note (the minimum denomination the cash machines dispensed) often left me feeling terribly guilty for reasons I couldn't quite identify. Occasionally, I would even be told that they simply couldn't make change and that they were sorry they couldn't do business with me. A 50 *złoty* note at the time was only worth about 20 US dollars. Several years later, though, this has become a less common problem.

The service culture in Poland was still recovering from the communist times when "bourgeois" restaurants gave way to cafeteria style, self service facilities, and any job was essentially obligatory labor. The situation has since returned to relative normalcy, and people generally get the idea that a business offering friendlier service will have more customers. But it takes time for cultural norms to completely change. It's worth remembering that the waitress serving your table or the cashier behind the counter probably receives a very low salary compared to the relatively high cost of living in the city. If he or she is a younger person, they may also be very well educated and a bit frustrated with the lack of work more suited to their particular qualifications.

To an American, the Polish people one encountered on the streets or in shops could occasionally come off as a little grumpy or impatient, but most were friendly enough and understanding when they realized I was a foreigner who spoke almost no Polish. Americans tend to smile more and go around with an overtly positive disposition – noticeably more so than Europeans, generally speaking. It's just a difference in cultural mentalities, and to a degree Americans can be perceived as a bit insincere or shallow as a result. At the end of the day, I think Americans really are just an easy-going, big-hearted people. Regardless, I've found that starting off with a smile in Poland usually earns one a smile in return, particularly among younger people who have grown up in a somewhat more optimistic country than that of older generations.

One demographic we were specifically advised to avoid were groups of young, male soccer fans at night for their brutish reputation and at times gang-like behavior. Their violent tendencies were usually directed at each other, but it was obviously best to keep clear of them. Aside from that, incidents of pick-pocketing and minor theft were not unheard of. Otherwise most parts of the city were quite safe. I felt at ease walking alone at night from the tram stop to the student dormitory along poorly lit backstreets. I would routinely pass young women confidently walking the same dark sidewalks on their own.

The *policja* (poh-leets-yah) was the national police force in Poland and a regular sight in heavily trafficked public areas. They might be considered a contemporary to the state police forces in the various States of the USA, but with authority spanning the entire country. Below that was the *straż miejska* (strahzh mee-ae-skah), the municipal forces of individual cities – though their authority appeared generally restricted to dealing with low level disorders in public places. A few recognizable private security firms were also noticeable here and there, with a security guard standing an intentionally visible watch in every little grocery store and retail shop to deter frequent occurrences of shoplifting. They might appear a little intimidating at times, but that's about the extent of their clout.

*****

Most Poles I spoke with – the majority university-aged – were curious to learn about me and the other students who had come from all over Europe and North America to learn Polish. Polish people very quickly opened up when I explained that I was an American of Polish origin and why I had come to Poland. The Poles' idolization of all things American may have cooled somewhat since gaining membership in the European Union, but the once heavily favored American cities of Chicago and New York retained sizeable communities of 20th Century Polish émigrés who still had connections with family back in Poland. I got the impression (one reinforced on future visits) that the United States maintained a pretty favorable standing in the minds of many Poles. The American standard was still seen as something positive, something desirable. American music was inescapably played in restaurants and malls, and Polish people often proved thoroughly versed in American film and television. At any rate, the warm welcome I received on that first visit made a lasting impression.

Being in modern Poland was a magical experience after everything I'd learned beforehand through my own studies in the States. With the exception of guided tours to Auschwitz and the Wieliczka (vee-el-eech-kah) Salt Mine arranged by the language school, I spent that first month in Kraków learning to pronounce Polish words, acquainting myself with Polish cuisine, and wandering around the city in the footsteps of national legends. Visiting Wawel Castle and seeing the tombs of the Polish kings and heroes about whom I'd read in the history books brought me closer than ever to a heritage my family had nearly lost.

Our somber excursion to the preserved Auschwitz-Birkenau death camp, built in Poland by the Nazi occupation force during World War Two

Chapter Three
Crossing the Country – Kraków, Warsaw, Gdańsk

Though I thoroughly enjoyed my time in Kraków, my impressions of Poland from that first month were only superficial. All too soon my language course came to an end. I knew one visit would not be enough. I wasn't quite sure how best to fulfill this growing passion for Poland, but I thought that seeing more of the country would be a good place to start. I returned later that year for another month-long stay. After renting a vacation flat in Kraków, I traveled to the capital of Warsaw in the east and the Baltic seaport of Gdańsk in the north. This second trip to the country gave me a broader perspective on modern Poland, helped to satisfy my fascination with Polish history, and insured that I would keep coming back again for more.

The sun set early over Poland in the colder months of autumn. Darkness arrived not long after 4:00 in the afternoon, the days growing shorter still as winter approached. Poland was at the eastern edge of the broad, continental European time zone which stretched as far west as Spain, making Poland's daylight period abnormally early. Geographically, the country might more naturally have fit within the Eastern European time zone of the Baltic States, Ukraine, and Romania. But Poland was tied to the West and kept time with Berlin, Paris, and Rome.

Vodka with beer chasers, hanging with Polish students

One evening while trying to contact some of my Polish friends from Kraków, I happened to be sitting in a quiet café across from a couple of university-aged Polish men. The place was relatively empty, so they invited me to have a drink with them. I cautiously accepted with a couple of preconceptions on my mind at the time – that it was almost impolite to decline an invitation to have a drink with someone in Poland, and that Polish men tended to drink rather heavily when they got started.

Once I introduced myself, they were quick to switch to English which they spoke fairly well. I was happy to find they were pleasant and welcoming – albeit heavy drinkers as I had suspected. Beer chasers followed vodka shots as several bottles of the latter disappeared with little help from me. My newfound friends were students hoping to one day work as engineers in the country's mining industry, a profession with a long tradition in Poland. They were curious, as most Poles tended to be, about my impressions of Poland and why I had chosen to come. We exchanged stories and soon began meeting regularly at that establishment during my stay.

Students attending university in Poland were usually expected to study for around 5 years. After passing their *matura* – an exit exam from high school necessary to proceed on to university – they would begin a 3-year undergraduate degree program. This was something like a 4-year bachelor's degree in the United States, but Polish students were then generally expected to work on a master's degree which took another two years to complete. As in the States, the Polish university system also offered PhD level studies in a variety of fields.

In America, however, a person with a 4-year degree would probably chose to acquire several years of work experience before thinking about the completion of a master's degree (though certain specialized fields like medicine or law required additional studies). Acquiring a post graduate degree was not always considered necessary since American employers were usually more interested in a person's proven work experience than in his academic credentials. This was a slightly different philosophy probably more suited to American culture than European society. The latter, I came to conclude, was more obsessive about academic titles than we were in the States. Europeans were more inclined to emphasize education for its own, altruistic value, while Americans tended to see education as a means to getting a better job. I would go on to meet a lot of European students who studied subjects which they found interesting, but who didn't really have a solid concept of how they wanted to apply that education once their studies were complete.

One thing I have always been impressed by while among European students was their linguistic education. Basic English was a fundamental in most European countries, with even the French (probably only grudgingly) acknowledging that English had become the common standard of international communication. The European Union being a patchwork of small countries speaking a multitude of languages, knowing some English was practically a necessity for international business and travel. Not only second but even third languages were sometimes learned to a moderate level of proficiency. My acquaintances at the bar in Kraków, however, offered a more personal explanation for their desire to learn English. They wanted to be able to watch American cartoons and sitcoms. Humor doesn't always translate well between languages, and they said that watching their favorite comedies in the original English versions was better than listening to the Polish translator talking over the actors' voices.

Polish patriotism

I happened to be in Poland on the 11th of November – Poland's Independence Day. The date corresponded with the end of World War One and the restoration of the Republic of Poland following 123 years under foreign rule. Amidst the chaos of World War One, the German and Austrian governments agreed to establish a limited Polish administration in an attempt to win the Pole's support, while Polish activists were working in the capitals of Britain, France, and the United States to raise the issue of Polish statehood in the West. Even US President Woodrow Wilson began championing the cause of an independent Poland as a necessary outcome of the war. As Russia descended into the Bolshevik Revolution and the German and Austro-Hungarian monarchies neared their ends, the opportunity came for the Polish people to claim control of their homeland once more. In short order, multiple political administrations declared themselves, and Józef Piłsudski – who had organized Polish military forces with Austrian support – assumed the role of Poland's top military commander and ultimately head of state. On November 11, 1918, modern Poland became an independent country.[19]

On Independence Day, Kraków's old town streets were decked with white and red banners – Poland's national colors – and practically every apartment building and townhouse displayed the Polish flag. Parades were common across the country on the 11th, and military uniforms representing various periods from Polish history accompanied marching bands and even traditional mounted cavalry clopping along the cobblestone streets of Kraków's old town. The procession led from Wawel Castle to the market square amidst crowds of flag-waiving spectators before making its way out the medieval Floriańska Gate. Poland having struggled so long for independence – both during the Partitions and later under Soviet domination – it was no surprise that 21st Century Poles tended to be overtly patriotic. During the communist period, the date of the national celebration was moved to July 22nd to mark the Polish communist manifesto proclaimed in 1944, but the traditional date of November 11th was restored when the communist system was overturned in 1989.

Poland's national anthem was the "*Mazurek Dąbrowskiego*" – in English "Dabrowski's March". It was also known by its most famous line, "Poland is not yet lost (as long as we still live)". It was written in 1797, not long after the fall of old Poland, to inspire Polish troops serving under General Dąbrowski in Napoleon Bonaparte's Polish Legions. Its message was meant to reassure the Poles that their country's foreign occupation was temporary and that Poland would ultimately be restored – a message which continued to resonate through the centuries which followed.

Poland's flag was also commonly hoisted around the country on the public holidays from May 1st through May 3rd. The 1st of May was May Day (International Workers Day) as well as the date Poland joined the European Union. May 3rd was Constitution Day, commemorating the first Polish constitution of 1791. May 2nd was established as Flag Day in 2004 to fill the gap between the two existing holidays. The 1st and the 3rd were the only official days off from work, but a lot of Poles would take a few extra days leave around those dates to gain a full week of vacation. Unfortunately, travelling within Poland during that week meant dealing with heavy traffic and crowded destinations.

There were also those who were less likely to participate in public displays of patriotism, given the sort of mandatory enthusiasm for the state and the heavy emphasis on symbols that existed during the communist years. Patriotism was redefined by the communists to mean supporting the communist order as they replaced old holidays with new, more "correct" ones and even appropriated such national icons as Chopin for the subtle delivery of propaganda[20]. Even in modern Poland, outward displays of patriotic spirit still felt somehow unnatural to some, stirring uncomfortable associations formed in years past.

Other people seemed to have simply grown weary of present-day politicians or social movements trying to associate themselves with certain historical events or tragedies. As in the United States, Polish patriotic expressions were often tied to the remembrance of important moments in history, especially those related to military conflicts. In Poland, however, there was a particular focus in politics and the media on the most painful events like the brutally crushed Warsaw Uprising of 1944, when Polish resistance fighters fought in vain to retake the country's capital from Nazi German forces; or the Katyń Massacre, the organized mass murder of thousands of Poles in 1940 at the hands of the Soviet secret police.

In the year following my second trip to Poland, commemorations of the tragic plane crash in Smolensk, Russia in 2010, which killed the president of Poland and other high ranking dignitaries (on their way to a ceremony commemorating the Katyń Massacre), actually turned into a source of division within Polish society, starting with disagreements over an appropriate memorial. The Smolensk crash became a heavily politicized rallying point for a group of conservative, Catholic Poles who presented themselves as the guardians of the Polish tradition, mixing patriotic as well as religious symbols with rightwing politics in opposition to the country's more moderate or secular influences[21]. Once again the politicization of patriotism, this time by the right, had the effect of pushing other Poles away from such patriotic expressions.

Other occasions when Polish flags came out tended to revolve around sporting events. Across Europe, soccer was followed with an almost religious fervor. Though for much of the year the local soccer teams were the focus in Poland, whenever a major international level event came up like the European Championship or the World Cup, the Polish flags came out again in support of the country's national team. People donned white-and-red-themed novelty hats and scarves and could be seen sporting Poland soccer jerseys on city streets.

Unfortunately, along with the passionate support for local soccer teams, Poland had fallen victim to a disturbing soccer hooligan culture which expressed itself in widespread vandalism and occasionally violent assaults on police forces attempting to contain the damage. Most fans were perfectly civil sports enthusiasts, but Poles have described to me large groups of the more troublesome supporters – numbering at times in the hundreds – occasionally moving en masse from one team's city to that of an opposing team to wreak havoc on match days. Kraków had even resorted to providing dedicated busses for certain groups of fans returning from matches to keep riotous passengers from ruining the interiors of the regular public transports. Kraków alone had two opposing soccer teams whose gang-like supporters seemed to be in a state of perpetual warfare with each other. The very public murder of one hooligan gang's leader by a group of machete-wielding assailants from another gang made grim headlines in 2011[22].

With uncivil behavior evoked by something as trivial as a game, it was no great surprise to see even politically oriented Independence Day demonstrations on the streets of Warsaw becoming increasingly violent. According to news reports, the cause in part was openly purported to be soccer hooligans who had infiltrated the already emotionally charged gatherings and taken the opportunity to spread further chaos[23]. There were clashes between opposing nationalist and anti-fascist marches in 2011, and clashes between far-right demonstrators and the police the following year. When it happened again in 2013[24], including the hurling of incendiaries at the Russian embassy and the burning of a gay tolerance display, it was clear that for a few, Poland's Independence Day had simply degenerated into an annual riot day when a small, violent element felt free to lash out from within a larger group of rightwing demonstrators.

For some, aggressive behavior obviously needed no particular cause to manifest itself once certain individuals learned to embrace a disregard for civilized society. Adding the uncompromising rhetoric of the far-right only inflamed an inherently volatile situation – with old prejudices confronting increasingly tolerant social norms, not to mention unfortunate circumstances of high unemployment among the young adult population[25]. It may be difficult for this particular group of Poles, who've grown up hearing constantly about their brave ancestors' many struggles for freedom, to see patriotism as anything other than conflict. Thus the only response they can offer to the challenges of modern society is to take to the streets in violent demonstrations that stir passions reminding them of uprisings against foreign occupations or repressive regimes.

Yet one can only wonder what young Polish children are thinking the Polish flag represents when they see it hoisted by an angry mob breaking windows, burning cars, and toppling street signs. Such mentalities seem far removed from the peaceful revolution of the Solidarity movement in the 1980s. Others in Poland have countered that patriotism in times of peace amounts to the ordinary responsibilities of the citizen toward his country, (admittedly less exhilarating notions) like participating in the democratic process, paying one's taxes, and being engaged in one's community – in addition to a healthy respect for the country's difficult but epic history[26].

Events in Kraków on Independence Day usually proceed without incident, but the situation in Warsaw overshadows everything else covered on the news that day. I have to contrast this atmosphere with that of Independence Day in the United States (July 4th), which features an overarching spirit of unity and pride, regardless of people's political perspectives. In America we see festive parades – during the daylight hours – attended by children – and of course the widespread American tradition of the backyard barbeque among friends and family. People end the day by turning out for fireworks displays which, again, are an opportunity for everybody to enjoy a national celebration that belongs to all of us.

The Austrian province of Galicia

My second trip to Kraków allowed me to continue exploring the city and its many layers of history. One brisk but sunny autumn day, I followed George Washington Avenue (*Aleja Jerzego Waszyngtona*) up a hill on the west side of Kraków and climbed to the top of the artificial mound dedicated to Thaddeus Kościuszko (kosh-choosh-koh). Kościuszko was an 18th Century military officer from the Polish-Lithuanian Commonwealth who traveled across the Atlantic to fight in the American Revolution. He served as one of the few professional engineers in the Continental Army of the new United States, planning defensive fortifications and conducting sabotage work which hampered opposing British forces. He returned home during the Polish-Lithuanian Commonwealth's twilight hours and led old Poland's final military struggle to retain its independence.

Reading his biography by Storozynski[27], I developed a great appreciation for Kościuszko. Though a low ranking member of the increasingly oligarchic Polish nobility, Kościuszko was a product of Enlightenment era thinking and inspired in part by the American version of republicanism which made (nearly) all men citizens. Opposed to black slavery in America and white serfdom back in Poland, he hoped that the Commonwealth's masses of peasantry could one day be educated to participate in a more democratic society. As Poland's enemies descended upon her, Kościuszko rallied the common people to take up arms and defend what they would come to realize was *their* country. In the end, however, old Poland was defeated by superior Russian forces, and Kościuszko's vision of a more democratic Poland was stamped out by the country's powerful, autocratic neighbors.

Kościuszko was eventually buried in Wawel Castle, but the Kościuszko Mound was built in his honor during the 19th Century Partitions of Poland from funds gathered throughout the three divisions of the former Polish-Lithuanian Commonwealth. The mound was a tall, grass-covered rise ringed by a redbrick wall and accented by a little chapel at its base. A narrow footpath wound its way up to the top of the hill where a paved viewing point offered visitors a panorama of the city.

Of the three foreign regimes which ruled a divided Poland through the 19th Century, modern Poles seemed to be the most forgiving of the late Austrian Empire (Austro-Hungarian Empire after 1867). Austro-Hungary was a collection of multiple ethnic nations and territories held together by the ruling Habsburg Monarchy's overarching bureaucratic regime[28]. Austro-Hungary's portion of old Poland stretched from Kraków into western Ukraine, a territory referred to as Galicia. Though it was said to be the poorest of Poland's three partitions – with masses of impoverished peasants trapped in a backwards agrarian society well into the industrial age – the Galicia region did gain a degree of political autonomy within the Austro-Hungarian Empire, and Galician Poles were not subjected to the level of official religious and cultural persecutions imposed within the German and Russian Partitions [29].

Southern parts of modern Poland adopted some loan words from the Austrians over the years, and the cuisine assimilated some characteristic tastes including spicy Hungarian dishes like lecso and goulash. In Kraków, reminders of the Austro-Hungarian period can be found not only in the city's many 19th Century buildings downtown, but also in the scores of fortifications built by the Austrian military in and around Kraków. In modern times, these were not always easy to find. The Austrian forts were often comprised of networks of tunnels and underground chambers dug into the sides of hills to provide protection from advancing artillery technology.

In the early 21st Century, many of these structures were collapsed and overgrown with vegetation, their condition unsuitable for receiving casual visitors. They were instead covered in graffiti and strewn with broken bottles, empty beer cans, and assorted rubbish deposited by random vagrants. Various plans would emerge to restore a number of the forts as museums or shopping centers, but until then their ruins remained tempting historical curiosities relatively unknown to most tourists passing through Kraków.

The overgrown ruins of former Austrian fortifications around Kraków

Traveling by rail

I soon continued on to Warsaw by train. Rail travel is certainly not a bad way to see more of the countryside, though it becomes a bit repetitive after a while. It does hold the benefit of being less stressful than driving on Poland's crowded country roads and having to contend with frequently discourteous motorists. Unfortunately, the standards of rail travel in Poland lagged a bit behind those in Western Europe. I've ridden the rails in Britain and Ireland and among Belgium, Holland, and Germany where there existed a whole other standard in rail comfort and speed. In my head I can still hear the rhythmic *cuh-chunck-cuh-chunck* of the Polish train cars rolling over each length of track.

At the time, the fastest train in Poland was the express line between Warsaw and Kraków. It took a little under 3 hours to go a respectable 180 miles (300 kilometers). Elsewhere, however, one could expect a roughly equivalent journey – say, Kraków to Wrocław or Warsaw to Gdańsk – to take many hours longer. The Warsaw-Kraków express line bypassed the smaller train stops along the way, often platforms of rusty steel and cracked concrete stained with dissolving minerals. If not for all the graffiti, at such stops one could easily imagine Cold War era scenes of Soviet soldiers in long coats and furry hats patrolling with Kalashnikovs. Maybe I exaggerate, but only a little. The mind does tend to wander when riding the trains.

Traditionally, train cars in Poland featured a corridor running along one side of the train and a row of passenger cabins along the other. Each cabin had two rows of seats facing each other, with as many as eight seat numbers assigned to each cabin. I've not actually seen eight people squeezed into one cabin – which would have been pretty tight – though I've heard it happens at times. I've been told that on occasion, the trains could be so crowded that people had to either stand in the narrow corridors or sit on the floor – not a very pleasant experience on what might be a six-hour ride.

Some trains were equipped with adequate heating

and air conditioning, but the rest could be cold in the winters and hot in the summers. It was thus important to dress for the environment. With all the windows open for ventilation in hot weather, the trip could be terribly noisy too. Sometimes it was hard to find soap in the lavatories. This wasn't really a problem, however, since running water in the restrooms could be equally hard to find. When riding with the TLK line, I was told in the ticket office that no reserved seating was available, yet when I boarded the train I found it nearly half empty for the duration of the journey. Nevertheless, the conductor charged me an extra 5 *złoty* for sitting down without a seat reservation.

Then there were the men who occasionally boarded the trains at various stops and went from cabin to cabin with a heavy backpack asking in each compartment, "*Piwo? Zimne piwo?*" They raced aboard and ran around trying to sell cold beers to the passengers before the conductor signaled the train was about to move again. As a more predictable and less illegal alternative, some of the train lines offered dining cars where hearty Polish cuisine was available at a fair price. Additionally, a steward made his way up and down the length of the train on some journeys pushing a cart full of snacks and beverages.

On the positive side, the ticket prices in Poland were lower than in the west of Europe. Naturally, the Polish railway infrastructure was undergoing a gradual evolution. While many smaller stops seemed to be either closing or inactive, making rail travel increasingly less convenient in this respect, between major destinations older trains were slowly being replaced with more modern designs. Plans for high speed rail were in the works too, though there would be disappointments early on as the costly, high speed trains imported from Italy could not be operated at their design speeds due to the inadequate capacity of the Polish tracks[30]

. Of course, I don't have anything to compare all of this to in the United States because where I come from, we simply don't have passenger rail service. People either take advantage of the far reaching interstate highway network or, for longer journeys, travel by air. Personally, I rather enjoy taking a train from time to time.

Warsaw, Poland's booming capital city

My trip to Warsaw crossed the Świętokrzyskie and Mazowieckie provinces where the scenery alternated continually between small villages and vast farmlands. Eventually, the distance between the little towns began to decrease. The smaller towns slowly meshed together until they were all absorbed collectively into the boundaries of the sprawling capital city. There were industrial areas here and there, and storage yards for construction materials or containers which had arrived by train from some distant seaport. We passed the suburbs made up of individual family houses, the big apartment blocks from the communist period, and increasingly modern apartment structures. The height of the buildings rose steadily as huge office buildings appeared.

I got off the train at Warszawa Centralna, Warsaw's subterranean central station. I emerged from the underground complex near the bubbly glass domes of the Golden Terraces (*Złote Terasy*) shopping mall amidst the city's growing collection of skyscrapers. Downtown Warsaw had a very different atmosphere from that of Kraków. Kraków had an antique charm to it, filled with street after street of original buildings from the 19th Century and earlier. Warsaw's city center with its towers of glass and steel had a modern, business-oriented feel, with its older historical sites near the river located some distance from the present day urban core.

While Kraków survived both world wars relatively intact, Warsaw had to be rebuilt in the late 1940s and 1950s after lying in ruins at the end of World War Two. Much of its architectural style was thus communist era design, but airing on the side of showmanship given the city's prominent status. Warsaw featured an underground metro for public transportation in addition to its street level tram and bus networks. At the time there was only one subway line, but a second would soon be under construction. Warsaw was Poland's most populous city, the center of national government, and the country's financial head. The Warsaw Stock Exchange could be found here along with the offices of various international and domestic companies like Coca-Cola, Dell, Ernst & Young, PKO Bank Polski, and Poland's state-controlled oil and gas company PGNiG. Most of these names could be found on some of the tallest buildings in the city center. The capital enjoyed the highest average salaries of any Polish city, with the prices of goods and services rising to commensurate levels.

Warsaw was a major center of education in Poland as well, with plenty of career options for graduates in business related fields. The University of Warsaw was Poland's largest institution of higher education. Other academic facilities included the Warsaw University of Technology, the Warsaw University of Economics, and the Medical University of Warsaw. The National Defense University of Warsaw schooled the country's military officers and civilian military experts. It could trace its roots to old Poland's School of Knights (*Szkoła Rycerska*) established in 1765, where Thaddeus Kościuszko was one of the first students[31].

The towering Palace of Culture and Science was a

dominant feature of the downtown skyline, and – to the top of its spire – the tallest building in Poland. It stood at the center of a vast plaza in the heart of the city. The palace's gray façade was fitting for a communist era design, while its decorative features like the whimsical little spires lining the cornices at each level and the grand columns surrounding the sprawling complex at the base were intentionally reminiscent of the renaissance architecture of old Poland.

The Palace of Culture was built in the early 1950s as a symbol of Soviet solidarity by workers sent to Poland from the Soviet Union. The design was related to that of several buildings in Moscow as well as to similar structures in the Czech Republic, Latvia, and an unfinished building in Ukraine. I couldn't help but notice certain stylistic parallels with the Empire State Building in New York City too. The palace's shady, Stalinist history aside, it was an impressive structure that had become a prominent symbol of Warsaw, and the viewing platform near the top gave visitors the opportunity to see the capital from on high.

I've heard people complain that the building didn't fit with the rest of the city, or that it was an unwelcome reminder of Soviet domination. But as a more and more diverse assortment of skyscrapers made their appearance on the Warsaw skyline, to me the Palace of Culture and Science didn't look particularly out of place. If people ever want to start tearing down reminders of communist repression, they'll have to flatten half the country, from the entire Nowa Huta district in Kraków to countless big apartment blocks in every Polish city. I realize there is a lot of sensitive history in Poland and I don't mean to anger anyone with these comments, but it just seems more sensible at this point to make peace with the past and move on. Today's generation of Poles ought to be able to look back from the comfort and security of their modern circumstances, and know that four decades of history were not entirely lost under communism – that their grandfathers and great-grandfathers did not labor and build in vain, as so much of the great city of Warsaw today will attest.

Central Warsaw's modern skyline, including the prominent Palace of Culture and Science on the right

I made the trek toward the old town, dragging my rolling suitcase behind me along the city's broad, downtown sidewalks. After a long walk, the sun quickly fading in the late afternoon, I reached the quarter near the Vistula River and booked a hotel room. My hotel overlooked the courtyard of a bright white, classically styled building where an honor guard marched back and forth and big, black Mercedes limousines pulled into the driveway with a police escort. I did a quick internet search to see who my rather official looking neighbors were only to discover that my hotel in fact towered above Poland's Presidential Palace.

The old town paralleling the river was mostly a post-war facsimile, but beautifully recreated from original photographs. These historic blocks were little more than crumbling brick walls and piles of rubble after all the damage done during World War Two, and their reconstruction was a noteworthy accomplishment of the communist years. In the center of the little market square stood a statue of the *syrenka*, a bare-breasted, mermaid-like river nymph bearing a sword and shield, long the traditional symbol of the city of Warsaw. The nearby "new town" – confusingly also a reconstructed part of old Warsaw – was another area filled with buildings retaining their original, antique appearance. Though the old town streets and the many traditional townhouses were far newer than their appearances suggested, their carefully restored details and slightly worn exteriors insisted to visitors that they were, indeed, walking along the historic streets of a charming old European city center.

The Royal Castle overlooked another square – actually more a triangular plaza – featuring a column dedicated to the troublesome King Sigismund III who moved the capital from Kraków to Warsaw. The reconstructed Royal Castle's exterior was dark orange in color, and the clock tower and corner cupolas were capped with copper-green, onion-shaped spires. The palace's baroque interior was complete with gilded halls and intricately paneled walls as much works of decorative art as those in genuine royal dwellings. Such was the level of craftsmanship that went into the restoration of old Warsaw.

Warsaw's Royal Castle (right) at the heart of the old town

The port city of Gdańsk, where a world war began and a cold war ended

My final destination on that second visit to Poland, after a lengthy train ride to the Baltic coast, was the seaside city of Gdańsk. Located in the northerly province of Pomorskie (poh-mor-ski-eh), Gdańsk would easily become one of my favorite Polish cities for its nautical atmosphere and its complex and pivotal history. Having grown up on an island and worked as a mariner for a time, I was naturally drawn to the sea and excited by big ships and maritime industry. For centuries Gdańsk was Poland's most important trading port through which vast quantities of grain from the inland territories of the Commonwealth were shipped off to Western European markets. Modern Gdańsk was still a functioning seaport and a component of Poland's shipbuilding industry.

As any good mariner would, I quickly headed down to the water's edge. On the way, I crossed the old town's Long Market. As with Warsaw, much of Gdańsk's traditional architecture was destroyed at the end of World War Two and had to be reconstructed in the years which followed. Beginning beneath the tower of the redbrick city hall building, the elongated market square was lined with tall, narrow townhouses in an assortment of pastel colors often sporting ornate pediments at their peaks. Reminiscent of old Dutch and Flemish architectural styles, some of these buildings were indeed the former residences of merchants from the Low Countries. Dutchmen did business in Gdańsk for several hundred years alongside their German, Polish, and Jewish counterparts in this once very multicultural city.

More narrow townhouses with steeply-pitched roofs lined the Motława River passage which flowed out to the Baltic Sea. A menacing wooden frame projecting out over the water from between a pair of cylindrical brick towers was a medieval loading crane which once serviced cargo vessels operating on the river. The museum ship *Sołdek*, the first freighter built in the Gdańsk shipyards following World War Two, was naturally one of my first stops together with the Polish Maritime Museum.

View along the river in Gdansk

After the Second Polish Republic emerged in 1918, disputes between Poland and Germany over the heavily German-populated city of Gdańsk (called Danzig in German) would help to provide the Nazis a pretext for war with Poland. The opening moves of World War Two included the Germans' surprise attack on Gdańsk's Polish garrison at Westerplatte. Almost 6 million Polish citizens died in the ensuing conflict, including 3 million Polish Jews who were slaughtered under the Nazis' ethnic extermination policies. Less commonly known, the Poles maintained one of the war's most impressive organized resistance movements – the *Armia Krajowa* or Home Army. Aside from direct assaults on German forces, Poles provided valuable intelligence to the Allies, including data on the German V2 rockets which were tested in occupied

Poland, and Polish cryptologists who escaped the country were instrumental in deciphering the German's vaunted Enigma Code. For a history buff like me, seeing where the war began was an important experience.[32]

The conclusion of World War Two left Soviet Russia in effective control of Poland's territory. The Russians subsequently installed a communist government in Warsaw which would remain beholden to Moscow for another four decades. The Polish communist leadership – an apparatus closely guided by Soviet overseers – was given the power to eliminate any potential opposition, and staged fraudulent elections to suggest that the communists held legitimate authority[33].

One elderly, ex-communist I spoke with a couple years later was of course quick to highlight the positive aspects of post-war Poland, noting how the country's cities and industries were rebuilt from their wartime ruins. A population subjected to years of brutality and fear were eager for the restoration of any sense of a normal life, and the poor people coming into the cities from the countryside found jobs constructing new urban living spaces and production centers. Various brands of socialism had been popular in Poland even before the war, and some hoped the future they were building under communism would indeed prove more socially just than the exploitation of the capitalists who'd recently delivered the hardships of the Great Depression. Popular enthusiasm waned however as the totalitarian nature of the new regime came to be quietly understood by ordinary Poles, and the last vestiges of independent enterprise were replaced by dysfunctional, centrally-planned economics.

Continuing my tour of Gdańsk, I remember walking along a somewhat overgrown sidewalk toward an increasingly industrial looking area where I eventually came across the Gdańsk shipyards. I watched as the yard workers and giant cranes assembled the massive hull sections of the latest freighter under construction there. These shipyards were the sight of multiple protests during the communist period including those of the famous Solidarity (*Solidarność*) trade union which sparked strikes across the country in the 1980s against the repressive communist order.

Under the leadership of Lech Wałęsa – an electrician by trade – and encouraged by the emboldening words of the Polish-born Pope John Paul II, the trade union's effort turned into a nationwide political manifestation which brought the communist government to the negotiating table. Events in Poland resonated throughout the Communist Bloc and were quickly followed by the toppling of the Berlin Wall and the collapse of the entire Soviet Union. As the Poles say, sometimes the wolf carries away, and sometimes they carry away the wolf. In other words, what goes around comes around.

*****

My second trip to Poland in 2009 gave me a chance to explore more of the country and to meet random Polish people through day-to-day happenstance. I toured the cities, visited the museums, and indulged my interest in Polish history. I enjoyed hanging out with the locals at the pub and chatting with a pretty Polish girl from Gdańsk who I rode with on the train. Before I'd even left, I think I was already determined to find a way to return for a longer stay. I never could have expected just how long my next visit to Poland would last.

Chapter Four
The Student Year, Part One

I applied to begin a year-long language program in 2011, once again with the Szkoła Języka (School of Language) at Jagiellonian University in Kraków. This time, I needed a student visa since Americans could only reside legally in the European Union for not more than 90 days in a 180-day period without official permission. I made an appointment with the Polish consulate in Chicago, and drove down from Northern Michigan to appear in person as required.

In Chicago, hearing people speaking Polish again certainly got me excited for my trip. A young couple with a baby, maybe US residents of Polish descent, were probably waiting in line to register their newborn's Polish identity, or to pick up its passport in order to visit relatives in Poland. A slightly older man and a somewhat younger woman were in line together, perhaps registering a recent marriage by the look of it. As for me, it took about 30 minutes to get a Polish visa in my passport – probably the shortest processing time existing in the Polish governmental bureaucracy. For US citizens, even the visa fee was waived.

Rest assured, the process for a Pole to obtain a visa from the American consulate in Poland was a far less pleasant experience. Poles could not enter the United States for any reason without paying a $160 visa fee and enduring a strenuous interview process. Poland was one of the few EU member states whose citizens were still required to obtain a visa to visit the USA even as a tourist. Evidently, Polish citizens had a high frequency of overstaying their legal visa periods in America. The Poles themselves have told me there was a sizeable underground of Polish migrants living and working illegally in the States, though most had arrived before Poland entered the EU and gained legal access to nearer labor markets.

Winter in Poland, smog over Kraków

I returned to Kraków in February of 2011 and got my first taste of the notorious Polish winter. I'd flown out of Chicago just after a major winter storm had blanketed the American Midwest in arctic-like conditions. I arrived in Poland to the sight of green grass surrounding the airfield. People assured me it was a mild winter by Poland's standards, but that I shouldn't expect to see any polar bears. As expected, the temperature ultimately plunged far below freezing. When it finally did snow, quite a few Polish women still confidently strutted around in high-heeled boots and short skirts (with very thick nylons I assume). Admittedly, there were some things I'd particularly missed about Poland.

The sky over Kraków seemed perpetually gray in winter – thanks in part to heavy smog levels from all the coal stoves in use around the city. Any day the sun managed to shine through was something to be thankful for. Those durable pigeons, of course, somehow failed to all freeze and die. How their spindly, naked little legs didn't crack off like icicles in the frigid weather was a mystery. Krakow's market square was quieter in the evenings than it had been during the warmer months, but the tour groups kept coming and locals and students still steadily crisscrossed the streets, trudging through biting cold winds or wet, slushy snow depending on the ups and downs of southern Poland's variable winter weather.

Krakow in winter, the snow-caked Planty park passing Jagiellonian University's Collegium Novum

After some searching for a location within walking distance of my language school, I rented an apartment in a townhouse – an antique, 4-storey *kamienica* (kah-mee-en-ee-tsah) with a view of Wawel Castle. Leaning out the window a bit, I could see my Polish-American hero, Kościuszko, in statue form above Wawel's gates. I'd found my apartment online through a housing agency which offered a dual-language contract (in Polish and English) to be sure I was getting a fair deal. The apartment building was old, probably dating from some time in the late 19th Century. Recent renovation work was a mix of retrofitted surface wiring, plumbing, and flooring supplemented by some second-hand furniture. The townhouses had high ceilings and thick walls of plaster-covered brick, yet they often remained poorly insulated. Mine had electric heating which wasn't cheap, but it was cleaner and more convenient than coal.

The apartment was one section of a larger dwelling which had once occupied the entire floor. It had been subdivided in the communist days, but was still quite spacious for a single person in the heart of the old town. I could tell from the fancy trim around the doors and the decorative sculpting on the ceiling over the stairway that the building had likely been quite elegant in its earlier years. I could imagine the now bare walls once decked with rows of old paintings in ornately-carved frames, the polished wood floors covered in colorful, hand-woven rugs, and a glossy-tiled coal stove filling the corner of the room more recently occupied by an electric space heater.

When spring came I was treated to a view over the blossoming *Planty* park, a forested green space which followed the path of the moat that once paralleled the old town's city walls. On a sunny day, the *Planty* was filled with colors – the smaller trees blooming with yellow and white foliage, the taller trees budding with a collage of light green leaves sprouting from dark, mossy branches. Tiny flowers carpeted the grass to either side of the paved walkway between the trees. After the long, gray winters, Cracovians eagerly emerged in large numbers to stroll the park once more, as soon as warmer weather restored the *Planty* to life.

The 1-year language course was more heavily weighted with Western European students than the one-month course I'd taken in 2009, but there were still quite a few foreigners with Polish roots like myself. There was also a noteworthy level of attendance from Asian countries – particularly South Korea. The atmosphere among the students was less party-oriented than during the summer course filled with American teenagers, but my multinational colleagues and I certainly enjoyed regular walks together after class to go for lunch or to enjoy a round of drinks in one of the many downtown garden cafés. Stepping in through the façades of the old town buildings often led one into the formerly private courtyards of the merchants and nobility. Their descendents and successors had since turned these once exclusive patios into restaurants and beer gardens.

My exploration of Polish traditions continued with "*Tłusty czwartek*" (twoo-stih chvahr-tek) or "Fat Thursday". The beginning of the traditional Catholic observance of Lent was celebrated with a multi-course meal and the eating of *pączki* (pownch-kee), sweet pastries filled with rose petal jam. I'd already become a fan of these little pastries back in the States thanks to the influence of the Polish-American community and the general American appreciation for jelly donuts with our morning coffees. Though I didn't personally participate in Lent, I was more than happy to join in this publically sanctioned gorging on pastries for a day.

For the Christian holy day of Palm Sunday, the Polish language school took us to the little town of Lipnica Murowana (leep-nee-tsah moor-oh-vah-nah) located not far to the southeast of Kraków. As with Kraków's market square on Palm Sunday, the Lipnica town square was adorned with columns of palm branches tied together into tall stalks and decorated with flowers and ribbons. Lipnica was known for hoisting an exceptionally tall palm stalk which reached around 100 feet (over 30 meters) in height. Vendors set up stalls selling craftworks and local culinary specialties like cheeses and sausages, and priests led a procession of children dressed in colorful Polish folk costumes from the church to the town square and back. The occasion also offered us a surprise opportunity to see Polish President Bronisław Komorowski who was in attendance for the traditional raising of the giant Lipnica palm.

The Polish Easter tradition included *święconka* (shvee-en-tsohn-kah), where Catholics would take bread and eggs in baskets to special church services to have the food blessed by their priests before the holiday. People would line the walkways leading into the churches and wait as the priests made their way past with aspergillum brushes to shake a bit of holy water onto the baskets. I would have to wait until the next year, though, to be included in this ritual by my Polish fiancée (more on that later). Aside from hardboiled eggs, Easter breakfast usually included the aforementioned *żurek* (my favorite sour soup) together with cold cuts and egg salads. The decorative painting of eggs – usually in very ornate patterns (*pisanki*) – is also a Polish tradition at Easter, a form of folk art with origins predating the Christian holiday but eventually assimilated into it.

Another curious Polish tradition called *Śmigus Dyngus* might be encountered on the Monday following Easter. Young boys eagerly awaited the opportunity to surprise the girls by splashing water on them, an old tradition with obscure origins. *Śmigus Dyngus*, known by other names, extended beyond Poland and probably had ancient Slavic roots. It seemed the prettiest girls tended to be the most heavily targeted (ancient Slavic origin of the wet t-shirt contest?), but the girls could have their revenge the next day when they got to soak the boys.

Southwestern Poland, from former German cities to the coal mines of Silesia

In the spring of 2011, I made my first exploratory trip out of Kraków for that year. Meeting up with a Polish friend of mine from Gliwice (glee-vee-tseh) who I had come to know on my first visit to the country, I took the long train ride from Kraków to Wrocław in Poland's southwest. The southwest of Poland bordering the Czech Republic was a region historically known as Silesia (Śląsk in Polish). In modern times, this can be a little confusing since Silesia is also the name of one of the three, present-day provinces of the broader Silesian region – namely, from west to east, Lower Silesia, Opole, and Silesia (or the last one also referred to as Upper Silesia). The Polish word for Silesia today is more commonly used in reference to the individual province of "Upper" Silesia.

The southwestern lands of modern Poland, stretching from Germany to Slovakia, have been parts of several kingdoms and states throughout their history. In medieval times falling within the Moravian and Bohemian realms which once existed in Central Europe, the region came under Polish rule around the late 10th Century. Its governance later passed among Bohemia, Austria, and Germany over the course of several centuries before being joined to modern Poland after World War Two. In modern times southwestern Poland was generally well developed and its provinces some of the wealthiest in the country.

The city of Wrocław (vrohts-wahv), together with the surrounding Lower Silesia province, spent much of its recent history within the borders of Germany. The Germans fought hard to keep the city in the waning days of World War Two, and Wrocław (or Breslau in German) suffered heavy damage as the Soviet Army pushed westward. After the war, Wrocław and the rest of Lower Silesia were transferred from Germany to Poland as compensation for lost Polish lands farther east that became parts of Ukraine, Belarus, and Lithuania.

Arriving downtown at the main railroad station gave us swift access to the historic city center. Like Kraków, central Wrocław was filled with colorful, antique buildings and alive with a steady circulation of tourists. The large market square rivaled that of Kraków's in size, though the center of Wrocław's plaza was filled with a cluster of townhouses, cafés, and shops. Wrocław's distinctive town hall building on the market square, a brownish brick structure rimmed with decorative gothic spires, was one of the city's most recognizable icons. Like most Polish cities, Wrocław's architecture was a mix of Old World European, communist era, and modern styles. One notable exception though was the Japanese Garden with its oriental motif. Located farther from the center, the Japanese Garden was a park area made up of tranquil ponds, little wooden footbridges, and exotic vegetation.

Wroclaw's market square (top) and iconic old town hall building (bottom)

Wrocław was also known for its curious collection of little bronze dwarves scattered around the old town. These statuettes usually stood less than a foot in height (less than 30 cm) and could be found carrying mail, repairing the sides of buildings, lounging around lazily, drinking, or engaging in general mischief. Stumbling onto them here and there quickly became a quaint amusement in itself.

I stayed at the residence of my Polish friend's parents in Gliwice that night, not making the return to Kraków until the following day. As I think back, that was probably my first experience with genuine Polish hospitality. Upon our arrival, my friend's mother almost immediately proposed a cup of tea, followed shortly thereafter by cake. Soon a full dinner spread appeared as we spent the evening chatting around the table before my friend and I went out for a couple beers in the city center. I've since come to see this as a pretty typical routine, confirming the Poles' reputation for hospitality was particularly focused on their guests being well fed.

It was also probably my first stay in refinished, communist era housing. The place was fairly small and I think the parents slept on the couch in the living room, but everything was comfortably furnished and brought up to a very contemporary standard. As was the standard in the old days, the toilet was in a small room separate from the bathroom. Furthermore, there was no shower curtain around the bathtub – another Polish norm – thus I should probably offer my apologies for any water that ended up on the floor as I tried to shower while seated...

Returning east by train toward Kraków, I passed once more across Upper Silesia. I would visit the area several weeks later, traveling this time by bus. While even outmoded rail travel in Poland could be the faster transport option in many areas where the roads were lacking, bus travel in this case was significantly quicker as the route was along a completed highway. Taking the intercity coach from Kraków, I was a little surprised though to see that when all the seats on the bus were filled, the driver continued to allow people to board and subsequently stand in the central aisle. They remained standing for the duration of the hour-long journey on the A4 highway. In the United States, for their own safety, passengers would never be allowed to stand while traveling at high speed in a motor coach on the highway. Actually, if they couldn't get a seat, Americans would probably never get on the bus to begin with.

Counting the entire population of its sprawling conglomeration of interconnected cities, Upper Silesia hosted a sizeable metropolitan area. At the core was the city of Katowice (kah-toh-vee-tseh), an urban center which actually felt rather American in scale, sporting plenty of wide avenues and high rises. Everything seemed very spread out even around the city center, more suited to automobile traffic and public transport than walking. While Polish communist architecture in general provided a slightly dated ambiance, Katowice was a Polish city with a relatively modern appearance. Only a few streets were lined with 19th Century townhouses, and the majority of the city center was made up of colossal housing blocks built from the 1950s onward. One of the most recognizable city icons was the Spodek, a large, multipurpose arena building resembling a giant flying saucer landed in the middle of Katowice.

Katowice's downtown avenues and high rises

Katowice came to prominence in the late 19th Century along with the development of the coal and steel industries in Upper Silesia. Being particularly rich in mineral resources, the Silesia area continued to be a major industrial center during and after the communist era, with greater diversification of the economy following the post-1989 transformation. The province was something of a regional melting pot in medieval times, so there were those in Silesia today who spoke with their own variant of the Polish language – something of a transition from Polish to Czech, mixing in some German influences. Though the arrival of a lot of standard Polish speakers over the past century has certainly thinned the Silesians' ranks, some young Silesians have told me that they still converse quite regularly among friends and family in the local dialect.

Others, however, have said they speak only standard Polish, with Silesian relegated mainly to the older generations.

Mountain excursions and Góralski hospitality

The next trip from my base of operations in Kraków was to the south near Poland's border with the Slovak Republic. Most of the boundary between Poland and Slovakia was mountainous. Poland's highest point was Mount Rysy at around 8,200 feet (or 2,500 meters), part of a chain of rocky, brownish-gray peaks located right on the edge of the country in the High Tatra Mountains. The Polish language school took us by bus to the lower, forested hills of the Pieniny range where we had a look at an old Hungarian castle and took a raft ride down the Dunajec (doon-eye-yets) River Gorge.

Niedzica (nee-eh-jee-tsah) Castle, situated above a lake created when the river was dammed, was the residence of several aristocratic Hungarian families for most of its history. Though the territory immediately to the south of modern Poland has long been a Slavic-speaking land, the region was mostly ruled by Hungary from about the 11th Century until the end of World War One and the emergence of the Czechoslovak state. The castle once served as an important frontier post on the Hungarian side of the border between the two allied powers of the Polish Crown and the Kingdom of Hungary. Today, Niedzica Castle finds itself on the Polish side of the Polish-Slovak frontier.

The scenic hills and rivers around Niedzica Castle

The local Poles known as the *Górale* (goor-ah-leh) or "Highlanders" lived throughout the hills and mountains lining the Czech, Slovak, and Polish borders. They had their own regional folk culture and sometimes spoke another variant of the Polish language – the Podhale dialect – which included vocabulary and pronunciation sounding a bit like their Slovakian neighbors' to the south. However, as with Silesians I've met, the younger generation of Highlanders has grown up speaking mainly standard Polish. One friend of mine with *Górale* roots told me her older family members could communicate in a language almost unintelligible to the rest of the family. Nevertheless, she was able to sing me a few folk songs which younger people still learned in the old *Góralski* tongue.

Traditionally, the Highlanders built wooden houses and churches in their densely forested hills, in contrast to the typical Polish architecture of brick and plaster. Their homes were topped with steeply pitched roofs to bear the weight of heavy mountain snowfall in winter. One of the most recognizable *Górale* specialties was *oscypek*, a smoked sheep cheese produced in little diamond-shaped rolls. This could easily be confused, however, with *gołka*, a more cylindrical cheese roll from cow's milk. Many Polish-Americans have Highlander roots, and the US consulate in Kraków offered their families in Poland quicker access to consular services than the long journey to the American embassy in Warsaw.

At the Dunajec River, Highlanders in traditional costumes with their black, round-topped hats floated us down the stream on wooden rafts. The *Górale* steered their unpowered craft using long poles which reached down to the shallow river bottom. The Dunajec flowed tranquilly, for the most part, but at a few narrow turns its pace quickened enough to splash spray up into the rafts. The gray canyon walls rose high above us at times, and at times fell away into gentle slopes covered in alternating light and dark green forestation. Following the river excursion, our *Górale* hosts prepared a roasted goat cooked over an open fire, and we dined at picnic tables in a little outdoor park.

*Raft ride down the Dunajec River with my fellow
Polish language students*

The Polish, Slovak, and Czech languages belong to the West Slavic branch of the Slavic language family. The Slavic languages spoken to the east of Poland including Belarusian, Ukrainian, and Russian constitute East Slavic, while the Slavic languages of the Balkans comprise the South Slavic branch. All three broader Slavic language branches share a common origin and some similarities in sounds, grammar, and vocabulary, but the three branches have drifted enough from each other over the ages to prevent them from being mutually intelligible in modern times. By comparison, English, Dutch, and German are all linguistically related, but far from interchangeable.

However, Poles have explained to me that the languages within the West Slavic branch – Polish, Slovak, and Czech – are close enough to allow some basic level of understanding. Although the Czechs and the Slovaks were joined together into the combined state of Czechoslovakia during the 20th Century, they continued to speak slightly differing languages which had to be learned if Czechs and Slovaks wanted to ensure full comprehension between themselves. Of the two, Slovakian is said to be more understandable from the perspective of a Polish speaker. Czech, in comparison, is farther from Polish and very difficult to interpret, though a Pole might at least get the underlying themes being spoken about by a Czech.

The highest peaks of the Tatra Mountains were just across the Slovak border. My Polish fiancée and I took a trip there later that year, drawn by the hot springs and thermal spas in a number of mountain villages. While there, I was happy to find that I could understand a bit of Slovakian even with my limited grasp of the Polish language. On the other hand, when traveling through the Czech Republic, while it seemed like the average cashier understood me when I spoke in simple Polish, we usually met with greater success by switching to English.

As a Polish language student, it was also worth noting that boarder changes and centuries of close contact between Poles and people in areas of Lithuania, Belarus, and Ukraine have left some Polish speakers behind. Quite a few Polish-speaking Lithuanians can still be found in and around the Lithuanian capital of Vilnius (called Wilno in Polish). On the territory of modern Belarus, where exactly Polish ended and Belarusian began was long a complicated matter until the Soviet Union undertook a program of ethnic cleansing during and after World War Two. Some Polish speakers nevertheless remained in Belarusian cities along the Polish border like Hrodna and Brest (Grodno and Brześć in Polish), though many Poles there found it necessary to adopt the Russian language during the Soviet era. While the Poles were mostly expelled from Ukraine after the Second World War, some people still spoke a variant of Polish in the western Ukrainian countryside around L'viv (Polish: Lwów). Most of my Polish language courses in Kraków have included Ukrainian students who had one or more Polish grandparents from that area.

Chapter Five
The Student Year, Part Two

In late May, the visitor to Kraków or various other Polish cities may run into a huge parade of university-aged people dressed up in all kinds of costumes – the more ridiculous the more fashionable. The horde of students descends upon the old town's main market square and is granted the "keys to the city" by the mayor (or president of the city, in Polish). In Kraków, the tradition dates back centuries and is known as *Juwenalia* (yoo-ven-ah-lee-ah). For several days, the students officially rule.

The most popular event in Kraków seemed to be the big party around the AGH University of Science and Technology. Revelers covered the large field amidst the university dormitories in picnic blankets and portable charcoal grills. And plenty of trash. Being in my late twenties, I was already feeling a bit out of place among college students in their late teens and early twenties, but it was a fun atmosphere filled with probably unhealthy food and drink, and definitely unhealthy decibels of sound coming from "the beach". The beach was a strip of parking lot temporarily transformed into a mock seaside concert area complete with sand, umbrella-covered tables, and smoky *kiełbasa* stands.

Weary partygoers simply returned to their dorm rooms once they'd had enough fun – or whatever dorm room they happened to find available, in some cases. I seem to recall waking up in a small bunk back in the Piast Dormitory with a Polish-American girl sleeping next to me and a Ukrainian girl curled up on my legs. It was all perfectly innocent, of course, as everyone was just dead tired by the end of the night. *Juwenalia* was one of those things I would probably only do once in a lifetime, but it was a traditional part of being a student in Kraków.

Getting to know the Polish girls, and date nights with Polish film

There was no escaping the fact that the majority of university-aged Polish women were uncommonly pretty. Polish women might seem a little reserved at first, but once they're sure what they want, there's no stopping them. Though Polish cultural attitudes tended to encourage traditional family roles for women, Polish women were frequently well educated and career oriented. Younger women usually had to work regardless to help pay the bills, and it was a common sight to see a child cared for during the day by its grandmother while the mother was away at work.

I wouldn't say that Polish women were attracted to foreign men more intensely than any other women in the world, but they certainly seemed curious. Being in a group of language students from all across Europe, it was commonplace to find myself at a party where most of the girls were young Polish students and most of the guys were a mix of foreigners. Regularly surrounded by such beauty, I naturally found myself searching for a companion to share in my exploration of the country and my efforts with the language.

It was in June of 2011 when I met one Polish woman who would dramatically change the course of my life – and take me deeper into the Polish world then I ever planned. From our first meeting, I could tell that she and I had exceptionally compatible personalities. She was native to Kraków and working as a project manager for an American company. She shared my enthusiasm for travel, and her English was excellent – a little too good as we would later come to realize since it was simply too convenient for us to converse in English rather than Polish. She still jokes from time to time that I need to find myself a Polish girlfriend who can help me to practice the language.

Very quickly we were spending most of our free time together, and it began to feel abnormal to be apart. We went out for drinks, watched a fireworks show over the Vistula River, enjoyed some live jazz in Kraków's clubs, and went for regular walks together around the *Planty* park near my apartment. We enjoyed bicycling as well, following the paved pathway along the river, or cruising the flat landscape of the downtown area until finding a café to stop in when we were ready for a break. We were always very comfortable together and it didn't take long for us to start talking about what the future might hold.

The first time my Polish girlfriend came to visit me at my downtown apartment, I learned that I had, for some time, probably been violating a traditional Polish custom related to guests. She had to ask me for a cup of tea when I failed to offer her one. I couldn't imagine why anyone would want a steaming cup of tea on a hot summer day, but worse still I had to inform her that I didn't have any tea. I wasn't a tea drinker and didn't keep any in my apartment. Whenever I wanted a cup of coffee, I went out for coffee at one of the many nearby cafés rather than sit alone at home. Apparently, the first thing people do in Poland when guests arrive is to offer them a warm beverage, just as my hosts in Gliwice had done earlier that year.

In the United States, one might offer a guest a hot cup of coffee on a cold day; but on a hot day, an American would more likely offer a guest a cold beverage with ice in it. This made perfect sense to the average American, but it seems Poles were actually told from a young age not to drink cold beverages. They'd come to believe this could cause sore throats and even problems with one's tonsils. When my American cousin and his wife and young children visited us at a later occasion, the waitress at a restaurant made sure to bring the children room-temperature drinks. She was careful to inform my cousins of this, assuming they would appreciate her thoughtful precaution. Being Americans, of course, my cousins had no idea why the waitress would go out of her way to provide warm colas.

My girlfriend knew I wanted to learn everything I could about life in Poland, so she was always watching for opportunities to point out the little things which were commonplace or general knowledge among Polish people. One of the first cultural inductions she initiated was some schooling in Polish film. I had already ordered a few Polish movies via the internet while in the States, including *Potop* (1974) and *Ogniem i Mieczem* (1999) – in English *The Deluge* and *With Fire and Sword* – films by director Jerzy Hoffman based on the epic novels of 19th Century Polish author Henryk Sienkiewicz. I had read one of Sienkiewicz's books (in English), and the movie versions offered colorful depictions of the old Polish-Lithuanian Commonwealth. *Katyń* (2007) by Andrzej Wajda was another film I'd seen, depicting the Soviet Union's attempts to decapitate Poland's leadership during World War Two through a mass execution and subsequent cover-up. I suppose being a guy with an interest in Polish history and military conflict, I was naturally drawn to this genre of cinema.

My girlfriend continued my cinematic tour with a number of commonly known Polish and Poland-related films. *Pan Tadeusz* (1999) was a lighthearted dramatization of Mickiewicz's 19ᵗʰ Century poem of the same title, set in Partitioned Poland. Roman Polański's *The Pianist* (2002) and Steven Spielberg's *Schindler's List* (1993) were poignant dramatizations of the brutality endured by the Jews in Poland during the Nazi occupation – Polański being of Polish origin and parts of *Schindler's List* actually filmed on location in Kraków. *Różyczka* (*Little Rose*) (2010), set during the communist era, was the story of a naive college girl pulled into the service of the former Polish secret police. She was instructed to seduce a professor suspected of "Zionist" sentiments during a period of anti-Semitic paranoia within the communist regime. The film illustrated the corrupt tactics the communist era secret police forces could employ against any Polish citizen suspected of anti-regime sentiments.

My girlfriend also introduced me to more comedic Polish works – particularly to romantic comedies which I admit were actually rather funny. I survived chick flicks like *Lejdis* (*Ladies*) (2008), *Nigdy w Życiu!* (*Never Ever!*) (2004), and *Nie Kłam, Kochanie* (*Don't Lie, Darling*) (2008). These were the sorts of films every good boyfriend has to endure, regardless of his nationality. They at least offered me a window into Polish humor and were a change of pace from the often dreary Polish historical dramas.

Dzień Świra (Day of the Wacko) (2002) was a cynical but pertinent take on the frustrations of ordinary life in Poland – or perhaps the frustrations Poles inflict upon themselves – as embodied in the life of an angry, middle-aged bachelor who finds himself irritated by everything in the mediocre world he sees around him. *Vinci* (2004) was a clever comedy set in Kraków, surrounding a couple of capers trying to steal Leonardo da Vinci's painting "Lady with an Ermine" from a Kraków museum. The film's director, Juliusz Machulski, had previously directed several movies recognized as Polish film legends. *Vabank* (1981) was another of his criminal comedies, this time set in Warsaw in the 1930s, featuring a safecracker who gets involved in a bank heist as a vendetta for an old friend wronged by a crooked banker.

Probably Machulski's biggest fame came from the 1984 Polish cult classic called *Seksmisja* (*Sex Mission*) about a couple of men who awake from a human hibernation experiment to find the future world inhabited exclusively by women. This 1980s sci-fi spoof garnered popularity among Poles for subtly criticizing the communist regime then in power, creating a fictitious, totalitarian world which the heroes of the film have to escape and then overthrow. As the movie was officially a work of science fiction, its messages for Solidarity era Poland managed to survive the communist censors.

Enchanted castle ruins and surviving Poland's roads

My girlfriend and I both enjoyed the magical atmosphere of castles, walking among old stone ruins which have witnessed centuries of passing history and the lives and struggles of generations. I've always been struck by the way time can turn what were once such influential places into little more than historical curiosities. These former fortresses and abodes of wealthy and powerful men now find themselves trodden under the feet of Japanese tour groups snapping photographs – a sort of reminder that all the works of man are vanity. As an American, castles were particularly appealing to me since we didn't have many of them in the United States. Growing up on Mackinac Island as a child, I remember playing around a rare example of a preserved, colonial era fortress built by the British in the late 18th Century.

On a cool morning in early summer, our first excursion together outside of Kraków was to some of the castles along the so-called "Trail of the Eagles' Nests" – a chain of around two dozen defensive fortifications northwest of Kraków, built mostly in the 14th Century by order of King Kazimierz the Great. Many of the castles along the Trail were ruined over the centuries due to wars and natural processes of decay. The mid 17th Century conflict with Sweden was particularly hard on these fortifications as the Swedes and their allied factions in Poland-Lithuania fought for control of the Commonwealth. Like many of Poland's charming little points of interest scattered around practically every corner of the country, any single locality might not seem like a destination in and of itself, but driving around to two or three could quickly fill up the day with plenty to see.

Some castles, like Ogrodzieniec (oh-grohd-zhen-ee-ets) were impressive ruined fortresses. Their crumbling, gray stonework seemed to grow out of massive rock outcroppings piercing the grassy landscape. Others like Pieskowa Skała (pee-ess-koh-vah skah-wah), though repeatedly destroyed by wars and fires, were rebuilt again and again by successive noble families and left in comparatively decent shape in modern times. For a couple of young lovers out exploring the Polish countryside by car, the café atop one of Pieskowa's towers overlooking the area's forested hills provided a romantic setting for a cup of coffee and a slice of pie.

Every little castle had its own story and it its local legends, like the closely spaced Bobolice (boh-boh-lee-tseh) and Mirów (meer-oov) Castles. Supposedly, an underground tunnel linking the two fortifications was once filled with the riches brought back from distant conquests in Russia. A "huge treasure" was discovered beneath Bobolice in the 19th Century, which seemed to indicate that the legend was true and that more treasure might still lie buried in some collapsed chamber or passageway[34].

The line of castles stretching northwest from Kraków led in the direction of the city of Częstochowa (cheh-stoh-ho-vah). The locality was perhaps best known as the home of the Jasna Góra Monastery, the most sacred pilgrimage site for Catholics in Poland. The monastery housed Poland's signature religious icon, the Black Madonna, a depiction of the Virgin Mary and Christ Child with unusually dark skin tones (hence the name of the icon). Such was the devotion of some modern Poles to this work of religious art that when I visited out of a sense of cultural obligation, the sanctuary was so packed that people could barely squeeze past each other to get a close look. Others crawled around behind it on their hands and knees in submissive reverence.

The Jasna Góra Monastery, built upon a fortified platform of heavy brick walls, famously withstood an intensive Swedish assault in the 17th Century, and its survival – credited to the Black Madonna icon – inspired Polish forces across the country. The Swedes, who had nearly succeeded in conquering the Polish-Lithuanian Commonwealth, were ultimately repelled, and the Holy Mother was proclaimed the "Queen of Poland" in tribute. On the other hand, given modern Sweden's level of development in comparison with that of Poland today, not to mention the Poles' love of IKEA (a very practical Swedish home furnishing brand), maybe siding with the Swedes wouldn't have turned out so bad in the end?

Travelling by car in Poland was the best way to see the many sites outside the cities, but it could often be a very frustrating experience. Much of Poland's road network during my first couple years in the country was clearly inadequate for the volume of traffic present. The scarcity of controlled access highways (motorways, freeways, or in Polish *autostrada*) between major cities was a significant infrastructure deficit. Connections with the capital of Warsaw from large population centers like Katowice, Kraków, and the Trójmiasto, and between other Polish cities were mostly on 2-lane roads. Crossing Poland by car took hours longer than it would take to cover a similar distance on the interstate highways of the United States or the *autobahn* of Germany. It was disheartening to drive so smoothly between big cities across Hungary, Slovakia, Austria, and the Czech Republic almost exclusively on highways only to be dumped onto crowded, secondary roads winding slowly through small towns upon crossing the Polish border.

Repair work on existing provincial roads was a common headache too. In this respect, the biggest disruption to traffic seemed to be when repairs on one road were timed to coincide with work on another nearby road, leaving drivers with no way to detour around the mess. The result was that huge stretches of countryside became gigantic traffic jams. We've sat through a 10-kilometer-long backup on the drive from Kraków to Przemyśl due to construction on the various roads between the two cities. It seemed as if no one was looking at the bigger picture, considering how traffic disruptions in one area might be multiplied by concurrent roadwork in a nearby area.

The same sort of problem occurred in Kraków when one busy avenue would be shut down for repairs at the same time as the nearest major alternative route. City planning related to automobiles in general looked like a situation where more needed to be done. Parking in particular was a problem in many parts of Kraków, with one of the most obvious issues being the authorization of construction of big apartment buildings without mandating that adequate parking be planned for residents. Simply assuming people would park their cars on the curb left many of Kraków's narrow residential streets especially difficult to navigate.

Downtown areas suffered from plenty of parking congestion as well, with narrow sidewalks crowded by parked automobiles and antique streets looking like used car lots. To be fair, city government was partly hamstrung by nationwide legislation suppressing the price of parking meters. With the prices of curbside parking artificially depressed below market levels, the city's own – comparatively expensive – underground parking held little appeal. While the city government couldn't control curbside parking costs, it did have the authority to limit the areas where parking was allowed. This, however, seemed not to be in the city's interest. A reduction in the number of curbside parking spaces would imply a reduction in city revenues since the prices of the existing spaces could not be raised to compensate. Meanwhile rising ticket prices for the city's tram and bus network weren't exactly encouraging people to switch to the well-developed public transportation services, leaving both downtown traffic and parking an ongoing challenge. Unfortunately, systemic frustrations will be a recurring theme in later pages of this book.

Pushy drivers only made a bad situation worse with a general lack of patience. I've been passed countless times in city traffic by inexplicably agitated drivers who immediately slammed on their brakes in front of me only to get one car length closer to the next stoplight. Certain Poles would arrive at the back of a traffic jam, turn down a side road, wind their way up a parallel street, and then try to inject themselves back into traffic at a point farther ahead, only to end up becoming the cause of the disruption to the flow of traffic in the process. I'm sure they thought themselves very clever, but in doing so demonstrated a complete disregard for everyone else.

Something to watch out for on Polish roads was aggressive drivers who wildly ignored speed limits, passed recklessly, and thought that racing up behind you on the highway and riding inches from your bumper while you were passing another vehicle was somehow a necessary driving behavior. Even when drivers were already handily exceeding the posted speed limits on 2-lane roads in the countryside, there were always other drivers unsatisfied who would attempt to pass – even if it meant forcing oncoming traffic to veer off onto the shoulder to avoid a collision. Naturally, such drivers can occasionally be encountered in the States as well, but in Poland they were quite predictably associated with young males driving German-model cars. I would only be speculating to explain why exactly this particular association occurred, but something about owning a BMW, Audi, or similar vehicle seemed to severely affect the mentality of many Polish motorists.

When driving in Poland, don't be surprised if someone takes offense at your driving style, or suggests one way or another that you've done something wrong. Even if you drive perfectly in accordance with the rules – in fact, especially if you drive in accordance with the rules – an irritated motorist may pull up alongside your car, signal for you to roll down your window, and proceed with a profanity-laced indictment of how you shouldn't be on the road. In Poland, there's always someone looking for the opportunity to teach you a lesson.

A lot of secondhand cars seemed to have

questionable histories, and in my search for a vehicle some years later, we encountered cars which were not so discretely touched-up after having been in some kind of an accident. Given some Poles' driving styles this was no big surprise, but plenty of cars were also imported from Western Europe already in such poor condition. Many advertisements for "slightly damaged" cars were for total wrecks in need of serious reconstructive surgery. Polish guys often prided themselves on being amateur mechanics – sometimes they actually were – so buying a damaged car and rebuilding it could be something of a hobby. I, however, was no such automotive enthusiast, and my first car in Poland was, as far as I could tell, an above board import with Belgian license plates.

Gasoline in Poland was significantly more expensive than in the United States. After converting from *złoty* to dollars and liters to gallons, the price in Poland for a gallon of gasoline was a couple dollars higher. Much of the price difference was the result of high taxes on fuel sales in Poland, amounting to roughly half the price of a given quantity of gasoline[35]. Depending on the average price of gasoline in the United States, state and federal taxes combined typically amounted to less than 15% of the total price of American gasoline[36]. Nevertheless, despite the Poles paying higher fuel taxes and receiving billions of euros in European Union funds for the roads, the quality of the roads and the development of the primary highway network was an area where Poland was still lagging – more than 20 years after the end of communism. Even highways scheduled to be completed in time to accommodate the international Euro 2012 soccer matches in some cases were not expected to be ready until 2013[37]. Apparently, poor management, inexplicably high materials costs, and the rampant bankruptcies of low-bid construction firms meant that the construction of a given section of Polish highway could end up costing more than an equivalent section in wealthier, Western European countries[38].

There are a couple things about driving in Poland which I prefer over the States. There are very few stop signs in Poland. Instead, yield signs at minor intersections make rolling stops perfectly acceptable in many cases, reducing the frustrating need to come to a complete halt even when it's clear that no cross traffic is present. Traffic lights in the United States have a cycle of green, yellow, red, and then green again. In Poland, the light cycle is green, yellow, red – an additional yellow – and then back to green. The extra yellow light before the green gives drivers a moment to prepare for acceleration, a useful alert particularly given that most automobiles in Poland have manual transmissions, an antiquated technology still commonplace across most of Europe. The stepped transition from red to green provides the driver time to ease off the clutch (though it still takes forever for a column of vehicles with manual transmissions to get moving at an intersection).

Other little things caught one's attention while driving around Poland. Across the country it was commonplace to see people selling locally farmed vegetables, as well as fruits and honey, at little stands beside the roads. Later in the summer, people also sold *kurki* (chanterelles), a variety of wild mushroom, yellow in color, which grows in Poland's forests and is something of a delicacy. More often than not, these roadside operations amounted to little more than a single farmer or his wife sitting beside a few boxes of vegetables on the ground or on the hood of a car. Yet the freshest, farm direct produce could be had from such vendors for a very fair price when in season. When it comes to the mushrooms, though, it's best to buy them only if you know what they're supposed to look like. Every year it seems like there's a widely-publicized case of someone poisoned by eating the wrong kind of mushroom.

Women in short skirts occasionally waiting alongside the roads, seemingly in the middle of nowhere, also apparently had something to sell. My girlfriend explained that they waited here and there for lonely truck drivers to come along in need of a few minutes of "companionship". A more shocking discovery to me was the giant Polish wasp. I first encountered this beast while my girlfriend and I were still in the city, stopping off in the suburbs on the south side of Kraków. We pulled into a driveway and were about to get out of the car when a monstrous, black-and-yellow-striped insect landed on the windshield directly in front of me. I may be exaggerating slightly, but this oversized hornet looked nearly as long as the palm of my hand. A quick flip of the windshield wipers dispatched the frightening creature, though I was still hesitant to step outside. While my girlfriend assured me this was a perfectly natural sight, I was certain Poland's giant wasps must have been a mutated byproduct of the Chernobyl nuclear accident in neighboring Ukraine.

My girlfriend and I travelled significantly farther from Kraków that first summer together, driving as far north as Gdańsk and stopping at various points of interest along the way. Perhaps the most impressive of all the castles in Poland was Malbork, to the southeast of Gdańsk. The massive, redbrick fortifications of Malbork Castle were built by the Teutonic Order in the late 13th Century. This army of Germanic knights – originating with the Crusades in the Holy Land – was invited by old Poland's rulers to forcibly "Christianize" the pagan Baltic peoples living throughout Poland's coastal regions and in neighboring Lithuania.

The knights forged a powerful, military state along the Baltic Sea, helping to spread German influence (and settlers) eastward across the north of old Poland and basing their center of administration at Malbork. The Order eventually came into conflict with Poland and the increasingly Christianized Lithuania as the latter grew to be Poland's closest ally. The Teutonic state suffered a crippling defeat at the Battle of Grunwald in 1410 by a joint Polish and Lithuanian army, and went into decline over the next few decades. Malbork fell to Poland and became one of many royal residences of the Polish kings. Historically, 1410 marked the rise of the Polish-Lithuanian alliance as the dominant power in Eastern Europe, but lightheartedly the Poles have told me they remember the date because it was the last time they beat the Germans in a war.

Malbork Castle in the north of Poland, the largest gothic fortification in Europe

Post-communism anticlimax, typical frustrations, and bad behavior

Getting to know more about Poland by spending time with my Polish girlfriend, I was coming to develop a better sense of how Poles saw their own country. Naturally, the passing tourist or even the temporary student will glean a different level of perspective than someone who has called Poland home for years. Polish people love to complain and criticize – I've even heard it described as a national pastime – but of course progress often does seem slow. Plenty of Poles have emigrated over the last decade, seeing little reason to wait any longer for their personal circumstances in Poland to eventually improve.

Though I'm still inclined to present Poland through a positive lens, it's important not to overlook the realities faced by many people. At the same time, it should also be recognized that critical, negative cultural attitudes can be a self-fulfilling prophecy at times, hindering successful reforms, disparaging any particular solutions proposed, and so readily condemning any setbacks that it may be difficult to learn from experience. Politics belongs somewhere in the following, but I'll save that topic for Chapter Seven.

Perhaps the old socialist model under communism offered people a minimum level of certainty in life – notably when it came to employment – but it obviously didn't provide them with much. It certainly wasn't a model based on individual liberty, social justice, or equality under the law. Most Poles seemed glad the old days under communism were over, but where exactly Poland was going left many unsure about the future. Individual liberty and market economics brought prosperity to some, but month-to-month the average Pole didn't have much money left to save after paying all the bills.

Meanwhile, the banks maintained a steady barrage of television advertisements offering easy credit for all one's materialistic desires, and household debt was a problem as people impatient for the good life tried to buy that lifestyle with a credit card. A lot of Poles were having trouble repaying home mortgages denominated in Swiss francs, a lending practice briefly popular in Poland which had disastrous consequences when the franc strengthened against the *złoty*. Housing prices were dauntingly high in comparison to average wages, and many young adults had no choice but to live with their parents in small urban apartments well into the start of their working years. Such difficulties doubtless contributed to projections for a disturbing population decline in the coming decades which would only make it more difficult for the government to meet its obligations to the next generation of pensioners[39].

As the euro zone debt crisis hit following the 2007-2008 financial crisis, Poland seemed to fair pretty well. A competitive labor market, strong domestic consumption, and the continuing disbursement of EU structural funds gave Poland an edge for a time, with Poland maintaining economic growth while the rest of Europe slid into recession[40]. The Polish government initially had room to increase spending rather than cutting as the more heavily indebted countries in the south of Europe were forced to do. Polish people were among the hardest working in Europe, accepting longer working hours and more flexible employment terms than their more westerly counterparts. The Polish economy slowed, however, as economic stagnation in Western Europe endured, and unemployment was on the rise. Poland's level of investment in research and development was far lower as a percentage[41] of its economy than in nearby Finland, Sweden, or Germany, and while Poland was producing plenty of skilled university graduates, there was often nowhere for them to apply their skills except outside the country.

I spent a fair amount of time around university-aged Poles. Mirroring conditions across much of Europe, it sounded like getting started in Poland after university could be very difficult. However, unlike in neighboring Germany where there was a strong emphasis on technical and vocational training, Poland was churning out university graduates on a mass production basis, and young people could easily find themselves overeducated for the low-paying jobs available to them. Moreover, students I've met in Poland often gravitated toward more humanistic or purely academic studies which didn't exactly help them to develop skills useful to potential employers. Coming from the United States – where attending university was an expensive prospect – it was easy to appreciate the widespread access to higher education in Poland, but even a fully-developed economy needs more skilled workers than masters of the sciences and PhDs[42]. If everyone expected to be a manager or an intellectual, who was left to actually work?

The answer, it seemed, was a lot of underemployed university graduates. One found master's degree holders working as sales clerks in shoe stores and receptionists at hotels. Universities are very protective of their faculties and government funding levels – in the United States too – and I've long suspected that they don't adequately emphasize to students the practical applications of particular degree programs. Was there really any point in having a master's degree in gardening? Will a person who has spent 5 years studying at university actually be willing to pick up a rake?

The enduring complexity of Poland's pervasive, post-communist government bureaucracy also provided the Poles plenty of opportunities to complain. I'll go more into my own personal experiences later (Chapters 8-9), but for now suffice to say it often wasn't a very user-friendly system. People could face a variety of unpleasant surprises and frustrations whenever something needed government approval. In the United States, we refer to government employees as "public servants". In Poland they're called "*urzędnicy*" (oo-zhend-nee-tsih) – loosely translated as "officials" but stemming from the word *rząd* (zhownd), meaning "government", "rule", or "order". Thus perhaps the language was lacking some automatic connotation of where the burden of responsibility should lie. Procedure governed above all, and the success of any given bureaucratic process wasn't really seen as the responsibility of the government. It was instead dependent upon the individual citizen's ability to decipher the unknown process, to conform his individual problem to that standardized process, and to move it forward via the correct sequence of applications. Any given failure to arrive at the outcome the individual needed could therefore be blamed on the unpreparedness of the applicant, and not on the bureaucracy itself.

Poles and Americans alike have a habit of complaining about their taxes, so a brief anecdote is worth mentioning as an example of the sorts of irritations people could face in Poland. Real estate transactions presented a myriad of government-induced complications, but one of the most surprising to me was a story from my girlfriend about a colleague who had purchased an old, rundown apartment in Warsaw. At the time of purchase, this friend paid what she thought was the appropriate sales tax – a percentage based on what her bank assessed was the value of the apartment. She then proceeded to spend tens of thousands of *złoty* remodeling the apartment, which subsequently raised its value.

Meanwhile, the Polish tax office – which had up to five years to decide if it was happy with the amount of taxes someone had paid – calculated the sales taxes due based on what it felt a property *should* have been sold for, regardless of the selling price or the value assessed by the buyer's bank. Sure enough, toward the end of the five year period following the purchase of the apartment, the tax office suddenly told the buyer that she had not paid enough taxes. Most disturbingly, the tax office appraised the value of the apartment based on its condition *after* she had remodeled it. She thus found herself liable to pay a sales tax on an apartment far more valuable than the one she had originally purchased years before. Such unpredictable headaches coming from the offices of the government surely made it unnecessarily difficult for individuals and businesses to plan major investments.

On the positive side, some things about taxes in Poland were quite agreeable. Among immediate family members there were no inheritance taxes, and family members could gift as much of their money to each other as they wanted as long as they declared the transfer of funds to the tax authorities. In the United States, the recipient of such transfers was heavily taxed regardless of whether or not the money had already been taxed at the time the giver originally earned it.

Property taxes were also negligent in Poland, while in the States they could amount to several thousand dollars per year for a typical family home, and increased as the property value in one's neighborhood rose. On the other hand, those property taxes in America went to fund services within one's community like schools, local police forces, and the maintenance of city streets. In Poland, cities were dependent on the central allocation of funds from income taxes based on where every individual was registered as residing. Thus when people moved into big cites from the countryside or small towns, if they failed to register their change of residence with the local tax office, the funding from their taxes would go to support services wherever they were previously registered.

Then there were the random little behavioral peculiarities I began to notice, and not just on the roads. While many Poles were exceedingly polite and agreeable people, for some, grabbing for every petty advantage and getting away with just a little bit more than the next person appeared to be the only way to get by in life. All too often it seemed like short-term opportunism and doing things just well enough to get by were overriding impulses. A frequent example was parking one's car on the curb next to the door even in a large parking garage rather than taking a legitimate parking space farther away. People have repeatedly cut in line ahead of me, obviously only pretending not to have noticed me. If an appointed date had been set to return a borrowed item, the burden would very quickly fall upon the lender to get it back. Supermarkets required a coin be inserted into their shopping carts as a deposit, ensuring that customers would actually return the carts to the designated areas and not leave them carelessly strewn across the parking lot. Not surprisingly, given all these circumstances, there were also those who were always on guard, constantly expecting others to cheat them, and possessing a sort of "serves you right" attitude toward anyone else's mistakes or failures.

For whatever reason, there were strong anti-social tendencies among some Poles. Certainly alcoholism was a problem, and 24-hour liquor shops on every second street corner in densely populated residential areas offered addicts an endless supply of self-destruction. I've seen young men in hoodies traversing a crosswalk on a red light and stopping in the middle of the street to make aggressive gestures toward oncoming vehicles. I came to realize the graffiti on the walls in very public places had a recurring theme to it – mostly the names of competing sports teams spray painted first by one team's fans, and then crossed off and re-sprayed by fans of the opposing team. People would continue to throw their garbage beside an already overflowing trash can on the sidewalk. The clever Pole might take his household trash and dump it somewhere in the woods rather than pay for urban garbage collection. If a person had a ground floor garden beneath a multi-storey apartment building, he'd constantly be cleaning up the cigarette butts and beer cans tossed down from the balconies of residents living higher up in the building. It was as if some people simply had an aversion to civil behavior, as if they'd flat out rejected it.

Household trash dumped in the woods, a common blight near populated areas

To try to put some of Poland's more visible problems into perspective, though, I would point out that dilapidated urban areas in big American cities could be downright dangerous at night due to high levels of criminal activity. In Europe, I've seen the sides of roadways even in the outlaying districts of a wealthy city like Paris blanketed with household trash from poorer neighborhoods. I remember traveling through the western German city of Düsseldorf by rail and passing by block after block of apartments plastered with graffiti. England's soccer hooligans probably wrote the book on bad sportsmanship. Unemployment was a serious problem in many European countries after the global economy stumbled in 2008; the United States has struggled with above normal levels too. How America will ultimately deal with its massive government debt also remains to be seen. The Poles may occasionally assume the world beyond their borders can only be better, but in reality they're not alone in many of the challenges they face. In the end, of course, it is how they choose to face those challenges which defines them.

Return to Poznań, where it all began

In August of 2011, my girlfriend and I finally travelled to Poznań to see the city in western Poland where much of my family had come from. Although I had considered studying in Poznań when I was contemplating my first visit to Poland, Kraków's history and my own uncertainty about what I was getting myself into led me to select the prominent language school for foreigners at Jagiellonian University. Afterwards, I had spent so much time travelling around the Kraków area and seeing some of the other famous sites throughout Poland that I had severely neglected a return to my family's point of origin.

Most of my Polish ancestors lived in the Wielkopolskie (vee-el-koh-pol-ski-eh) province, the birthplace of the Polish nation. Over a thousand years ago, the Poznań area was the territory of the West Slavic tribe called the Polans, from which the name of the Poles and their country were derived. The Catholic baptism of the Polans' ruler, Mieszko (mee-esh-koh), in 966 is considered the founding date of old Poland. Following his association with Catholicism, Mieszko went on to bring several neighboring Slavic tribes under his rule, forming the early Polish state.[43]

As Mieszko's Poland forged its political ties with the Church of Rome, Poznań became the seat of Poland's first bishop and the site of the country's first cathedral. Though Poland's center of power would soon shift to Kraków, Poznań's location within the Polish-Lithuanian Commonwealth along major trading routes made it an important commercial center – notably a hub in the fur trade which my Great-great grandpa Jan Błażejczyk would become involved in centuries later. As a part of the German Partition of Poland, Polish investors in Poznań still managed accomplishments like the building of the elegant Raczyński Library and the founding of the Cegielski Company which manufactured heavy machinery like tractors and locomotives. During the communist era, Poznań saw further expansion and industrialization, but also protests against the shortcomings of the communist system as early as 1956.

At the start of the 21st Century, a cluster of high-rises comprised of offices, hotels, apartment buildings, and the tower of the Poznań University of Economics had risen above the area to the southwest of the old town. The city's streets and public spaces were well kept, and Poznań's strategic location roughly halfway between Warsaw and Berlin meant it continued to be a prominent center for business and trade just as it was hundreds of years ago. Together with the University of Economics, the Adam Mickiewicz University and Poznań University of Technology offered a ready supply of advanced graduates to businesses looking for a place to set up operations. Nevertheless, Poznań seemed to be in something of a competition for talent with the traditional educational center of Kraków. I would later see billboard advertisements in Kraków suggesting that graduates willing to relocate to Poznań would easily find employment there.

After touring downtown Poznań, we walked east from the old town center and crossed the Chrobry Bridge to see Poznań's historic cathedral. It sat upon an island in the middle of the Warta River which was once the central stronghold of early Poznań. Down in the cathedral's crypt, a subterranean chamber featured a catwalk suspended above an earthen floor. Protruding from the pool of dirt in the center of the chamber were the ruins of a stone tomb traditionally held to be that of Poland's early ruler Mieszko, or perhaps that of his son and the country's first king, Bolesław Chrobry. I couldn't escape the sense that I was in close communion with the very foundations of old Poland.

Poznan's historic cathedral, thought to be built atop the tomb of Poland's founder, Mieszko I

My girlfriend and I dined at an outdoor café on the market square that evening and met with another Polish friend who was in the city on business. The old square was a lively place dominated by a white town hall building and ringed by a colorful assortment of antique townhouses. The atmosphere was charming and inviting, and I certainly felt a natural attraction to Poznań thanks to my family history. I spent the next day roaming the old town streets and inspecting the local history museum located in the retired town hall. As I viewed the images of famous figures from the city's past, I found myself wondering if any of my ancestors had seen those faces in person.

Poznan's old market square and former town hall

I had completed the circle, returned to Poznań from

the New World, and quite literally walked in the footsteps of my Polish ancestors. Perhaps that was why I had delayed visiting Poznań up until then. In doing so, what was left for me to accomplish in Poland? Had I not seen everything I had set out to rediscover?

*****

As the months passed back in Kraków, I began to feel a growing sense of uncertainty. As the end of my second semester of studies grew steadily nearer, the question of what lay ahead weighed heavily. I spent weeks pondering everything I had learned, everything I had experienced, that lingering feeling of connection which had drawn me back to Poland. Returning to the States would have meant going home, but after spending almost a year in Poland I had grown quite accustomed to life in my ancestral homeland. I wasn't ready to make Ogiński's polonaise *"Farewell to the Fatherland"* my anthem.

There was, of course, the Polish woman with whom I had fallen so quickly and so deeply in love. It was through her steady companionship that I truly began to experience the fullness of Polish life and culture, to see the country and the people through the eyes of a native Pole – both the good and the bad. After a long, contemplative walk one dark, November night, I finally realized where I needed to be.

On November 28, 2011 I took my Polish girlfriend up to the courtyard of Wawel Castle. We had visited so many other Polish castles outside Kraków, we were surprised to realize we had not yet toured Wawel together in the time we had known each other. She thought we were simply going for another one of our typical castle dates. It was in the center of the courtyard of the Polish kings, largely empty on a cold but intermittently sunny November afternoon, where I knelt down and asked her to marry me. I started out nervous, naturally, but her swift acceptance was invigorating. We hadn't known each other for very long, yet it seemed to both of us as though this moment had been forever in coming.

Chapter Six
Joining the Family

We joked that not long after proposing, I had to live up to the old Anglo-American marriage commitment of "for better or for worse" when my fiancée sprained her foot. Since the elevator in her apartment building was being replaced and out of commission, I basically had to carry her down eight flights of stairs to the ground level. Following that, I got my first experience with the public healthcare system in Poland.

We proceeded to the emergency medical clinic where we waited patiently in line behind homeless people and the excessively inebriated that Sunday evening. My fiancée may well have been the only patient in the building actually paying into the national healthcare system. The building was old and worn, essentially standard communist period decor accented by indistinct indications of recent renovations. I remember they gave us a wheelchair so I could push my fiancée to another section of the building for an X-ray. We followed the photocopied signs on the walls directing us out the side exit and across the outdoor ambulance parking area – in December. There were no automatic doors, so it was something of a challenge to wheel her around. It didn't help that both wheels on the wheelchair were flat. A sign on the back of the chair had the English loan word "SORRY" written on it. We concluded it must have been the name of the wheelchair.

We were lucky that time, as she eventually got the attention she needed. On other occasions, we ran into the typical bureaucratic mindset prevailing within the system – if you come with a problem, you are a burden to the system. If a patient's injury was not caused within the last

24 hours, it was not considered to be an emergency. Thus, when she injured her wrist while on vacation and it began to swell painfully several days later upon returning to Kraków, she was refused help when we went to the emergency room. Clearly, if she had lived with the injury for several days, the official attitude was that she could live with it for another couple weeks while she waited in line for a regular doctor's appointment. The way the system worked, she would have to have lied about the timeframe of the injury in order to get immediate help for such a problem. She was therefore understandably frustrated to see so much deducted from her salary for public healthcare only to be turned away on the rare occasions that she actually needed to use it.

For me, using medical care in a foreign country could be a little intimidating at times, not being fluent in the language and not always being clear about what was going on. Doctors in Poland sometimes had a very clinical attitude toward their patients, speaking condescendingly and talking to patients in the third person – literally "he sits," "he stands," "he sticks out his tongue." Fortunately, those doctors who I've had contact with seemed to appreciate the fact that I was a foreigner, and tended to be more patient and empathetic with me. It was a curious contrast to the typical treatment which I've observed Poles receiving from Polish medical staff on more than one occasion.

Generally speaking, I've had distinctly more positive experiences with private healthcare in Poland. My fiancée had private health insurance too and could have easily gotten a higher standard of service when she sprained her foot, but only on a weekday. With private providers we usually had no trouble booking appointments almost immediately. Private doctors were typically very punctual – something rare even in the United States. The clinics were clean and modern, the staff courteous, and the whole experience comparatively timely and efficient. In some clinics, I was even able to indicate in advance that I would like the appointment to be conducted in English.

Unfortunately, private insurance in Poland was only available for basic services like medical screenings and outpatient procedures. More intensive procedures and any sort of long term care were only available from the state system. To make matters worse, the government taxed private insurance policies like income – despite the fact that anyone using private care was lowering the cost to the public healthcare system by choosing not to use it (while still being obligated to pay into the public system from their salaries). Poland's healthcare model compared pretty poorly with others in Europe[44], but was perhaps reflective of the country's overall economic standing. When someone in Poland developed a serious problem like cancer and couldn't wait for the public system to get around to dealing with it, I've heard of Poles moving to neighboring Germany to take advantage of what my German friends have told me is an excellent public-private health system there.

Christmas traditions and meeting the in-laws

Starting in early December, the main square in Kraków was adorned with glittering Christmas decorations and a festive holiday market. Little wooden kiosks were set up outside, and dozens of shivering vendors offered their hand-painted Christmas ornaments and crafts, grilled sausages, traditional cheeses from the mountains, and – a personal Polish favorite of mine – *grzaniec* (gzhah-nee-ets). *Grzaniec* is a mulled wine, a sweet, red wine with spices added and served hot. It's a southern Polish or "Galician" specialty, and on a snowy winter day while perusing the offerings on the market, it's a tasty alternative to a bitter cup of coffee.

Another Kraków tradition was the building of *szopki* (shohp-kee). These were handmade nativity crèches, but bearing little intended resemblance to the traditional Christmas nativity scene. Instead of the classical models of Christ born in a humble stable, for the sake of artistic creativity the *szopki* usually set the birthplace in a grand and fanciful cathedral fashioned from cardstock and shiny, multicolored foils. Officially, the designs were styled after the Mariacki Church on Kraków's market square, though they were usually far more exotic with multiple towers, onion shaped spires, and gilded domes – the more ornate and colorful the better. Each year, the completed models were entered into a competition for the most elaborate designs.

Szopki on display at the Historical Museum of Krakow

In the United States people often hung their Christmas lights and other decorations shortly after the American Thanksgiving holiday in late November. According to my fiancée, Poles typically waited until just before Christmas – sometimes even on Christmas Eve – considering the earlier, American Christmas season to be overly hyped and commercialized. On the other hand, as I pointed out in retort, while Americans usually took down their decorations around New Years, Poles often didn't get around to taking their Christmas lights down until February.

Traditionally, the Polish Christmas was less likely to include Santa Claus than the more heavily commercialized American version. Christmas in the United States featured waking up on December 25th and rushing out to the Christmas tree to open a pile of presents "from Santa" before perhaps moving on to church services and gatherings with the extended family. In Poland, Christmas Eve and Christmas day were mostly reserved for religious and family gatherings, while gift giving took place on the 6th of December – Saint Nicolas' Day.

When my fiancée was a child, Saint Nicholas – or *Święty Mikołaj* (shvee-ehn-tih mee-koh-why) in Polish – used to look like a bishop, but he has gradually morphed into the jolly old fat man in a red suit invented by the Coca-Cola Corporation and popularized in American movies. Children used to receive candies or chocolates under their pillows on Saint Nicolas' Day, but this has been expanding to include more diverse (and more expensive) presents. The traditions varied by region and often from one household to another. For example, exchanging presents on Christmas Eve instead of the 6th of December was called *Gwiazdor* (after "Father Christmas") around Wielkopolska and Kashubia, while Christmas Eve gift giving was called *Aniołek* (little angel) or *Gwiazdka* (little star) in other parts of the country.

Just as in the States, shopping centers were bustling almost constantly through December. Probably taking advantage of the confusion about when to exchange Christmas gifts in Poland, it looked like the marketing gurus had convinced Poles that at least *two* gift giving holidays were now necessary – both the 6th and the 24th of December. And it wasn't just presents people seemed to be buying in excess, but also huge amounts of food. The lines at the supermarkets grew steadily longer as December progressed, approaching a crescendo in the few days before Christmas Eve. At all hours, shopping carts filled to the brims with edibles formed disorganized lines extending far from the checkout counters. It was as if people who'd been dieting all year finally started eating again, and flooded into the supermarkets where they'd not shopped since the preceding Christmas season.

Soon enough, it was time to meet my fiancée's family. I felt I was pretty well prepared. I didn't consider myself a young man, at 28 years of age, and I was already quite accustomed to struggling through conversations with native Poles using a mix of Polish and English. My fiancée had already told her parents everything she knew about me. Her father had put me at ease by laughing off the notion of a formal request being needed for permission to marry his daughter, so we were free to enjoy our meal together with a minimum of awkward interactions. I recall the service at the restaurant we were meeting in being more stressing than the occasion itself.

Polish families are often close, and becoming a member of the family meant diving even deeper into Polish tradition. That Christmas, I got to experience a Polish Christmas Eve dinner, called *Wigilia* (vee-ghee-lee-ah), with my fiancée's parents and grandmother from Kraków. They served 12 different dishes – the number of Christ's apostles – which started with the breaking and sharing of wafers (*opłatek*). Each person would go around to every other in the room and take a piece of the other's *opłatek* while wishing a Merry Christmas and good tidings in the New Year. The evening continued with a dumpling-filled red borscht soup, the aforementioned *pierogi*, a cabbage stew with mushrooms, and various other Polish specialties. An empty place was usually left at the dinner table in case of an unexpected guest. It was a reminder of the Polish tradition of hospitality and of the lack of lodging for Christ's earthly parents who were forced to sleep in a stable on the night of His birth.

At some point, the carp appeared on the table. This was another time-honored Polish Christmas "tradition". Though it has been my observation that people eating this bony fish seemed to force it down more out of a sense of duty than any real culinary appreciation, there were those who adored this difficult-to-consume specialty. Every December, the supermarkets hauled out hot-tub-sized tanks full of live carp, and Poles across the country would carry home these flopping, squirming creatures and keep them alive in their bathtubs until Christmas Eve – yes, literally in their bathtubs. I've also heard a number of stories from Poles about wives or young children pleading with the head of the household on Christmas Eve not to dispense with the fish, as it had somehow become akin to a family pet. I was told that bringing home the live carp for Christmas was becoming less common, but apparently the freshest carp was the best.

My fiancée's father's side of the family came from the Kraków area, but her mother came from the pretty southeastern city of Przemyśl (pzheh-mih-shl) only a few kilometers from the present-day Ukrainian border. We drove to Przemyśl just after Christmas where I would meet the rest of the future in-laws including aunts, uncles, and cousins. They all usually traveled to Przemyśl for the holiday and stayed at the grandparents' large townhouse.

I was actually a bit more stressed about this introduction than the previous meeting with the parents. My fiancée spoke English fluently and her parents reasonably well. In Przemyśl I knew I would be completely immersed in the Polish language, which for me was still very difficult. Additionally, I'd heard that people from the east of Poland were generally very traditional Polish Catholics, so I really didn't know how well a foreigner and a Protestant like me would be received.

Though today Przemyśl is located practically on the border with Ukraine, it was once a busy trading center much deeper within the core of Polish territory. Much of what lies beyond the modern frontier was once a part of old Poland's vast Ruskie province. After the partitions of the Polish-Lithuanian Commonwealth, the city came under Austrian administration and saw the building of an extensive network of fortifications atop the surrounding hills. Przemyśl's strategic location not far from Tsarist Russia looming to the east made it a vital stronghold in the Austro-Hungarian Empire's defenses. Many of the city's downtown façades parallel the elegant style applied in Kraków during that period. Przemyśl became part of a restored Poland again with the end of World War One, but the Second World War saw the mass murder of the city's large Jewish community under the Nazi occupation. Przemyśl served as a provincial capital during the latter years of the communist period, but this responsibility has since returned to the larger, nearby city of Rzeszów (zheh-shoov).

Modern Przemyśl remained a relaxing, walkable town, pleasing to the eye with a charm that beckoned the return of anyone who'd had the privilege of visiting. The city was situated along both sides the River San, with older townhouses lining the banks, and newer, communist period blocks and modern homes expanding up the side of the valley opposite the old town. The locals filled the streets on a fair summer's day, but after a visit to Przemyśl the bustling metropolis of Kraków suddenly seemed overrun with tourists.

Przemysl's charming old town streets

In the end, I received a warm welcome from my fiancée's relatives and confirmed once again that the Polish reputation for hospitality was well deserved. Her grandfather – when he heard that some of my Polish ancestors were named Brzeziński – was eager to point out the Brzeziński family home in Przemyśl where Zbigniew Brzeziński had lived briefly as a child. Polish-born, Brzeziński would later become a citizen of the United States and serve as President Jimmy Carter's national security advisor and a key architect of America's Cold War strategy. Of course, I couldn't say whether or not these Brzezińskis had any relation to the Brzezińskis among my own ancestors from the west of Poland.

The atmosphere at the home of my fiancée's grandparents was festive since we were there for the

Christmas holiday, and an all-day feast was a prominent feature of the family's Christmas tradition. Polish grandmothers, like most other grandmothers I know, will do their very best to stuff you full of food at any occasion. An empty plate immediately summons another portion. It's a good idea to pace yourself if attending a large family meal in Poland. Some Polish guests will turn down an offered food or beverage item initially just to be polite, knowing the host will offer it again a little later. When Americans say they've had enough they usually mean it, thus my fiancée had to translate from time to time that I had genuinely eaten my fill.

Alcohol consumption, moderate or otherwise, is rather common at any social event in Poland, so opening up a bottle of vodka at a holiday meal shouldn't come as a surprise. Often this is accompanied by a few bottles of wine for those who don't have a taste for stronger spirits. In the States, typically prudish Protestants would consider it a little inappropriate to drink on a religious holiday. Even the taking of wine at communion in America had widely been replaced by non-alcoholic grape juice. In Poland, abstaining from alcohol would probably only occur during Lent, if ever. As the afternoon of snacking on cold cuts and salads progressed into the evening, the dining room grew louder and louder, the laughter moving in increasingly intensive waves from one end of the table to the other. The noise reached a peak whenever someone would hail, "*zdroovkah!*" – a call for everyone with a glass to have another sip.

Religion

Politics and religion are topics often politely avoided in the United States when introduced to new people at social gatherings. Naturally, among Poles these were some of the first subjects to come up when meeting my fiancée's relatives. Understandably I suppose, they were curious about this Protestant American wanting to marry into the family. I was baptized into the Episcopal (Anglican) Church, and also spent quite a few years in humble little Baptist congregations. My fiancée's fervently Catholic grandmother had the most questions for me, but I hope I offered her adequate assurance that I wasn't some sort of radical. I think her impression of Baptist churches was of people dancing in the aisles as the preacher shouted from the pulpit. She probably had us confused with Pentecostals.

Compared to much of Western Europe, Poland was a very outwardly religious country. A cross hung above the door in Poland's parliamentary chamber, and officials right up to the country's president could routinely be seen praying publically beside members of the clergy at official ceremonies. Religious adherence in Poland was overwhelmingly Latin-Rite Roman Catholic. Over 85%[45] of modern Poland's population belonged to the Church of Rome – at least by tradition if not in terms of active adherence. Catholic indoctrination even took place in public schools if parents didn't chose to have their children opt out of such classes.

For many, Poland's association with Catholicism was integrally linked with their concept of Polish nationhood. After all, the country's history officially begins upon the baptism of early Polish ruler Mieszko I into the Catholic faith. Surviving the 19th Century Partitions and 20th Century communist rule, the Catholic Church remained a steady source of comfort for the Poles living under successive foreign and atheist regimes, in essence the one thing the Polish people could truly claim as their own. Certainly the selection of Karol Wojtyła, a Pole from Wadowice, as Pope John Paul II was a turning point in the minds of many Polish Catholics who could finally look beyond their despised communist leaders for guidance. To this day, despite the succession of later popes, the Poles still refer to John Paul II as "our pope". Catholic doctrine thus remains a guiding philosophy in the daily lives of many Poles.

Protestant denominations were sparsely represented. The Lutheran Augsburg Church had the greatest following with roughly 60,000 adherents located mainly in the southwesterly province of Silesia[46]. A variety of other Protestant denominations were dispersed in smaller numbers throughout the country. While Poland's 16th Century Protestant Reformation saw the conversion of many among the nobility around the time of old Poland's Golden Age, the movement failed to spread to the bulk of the peasantry and thus to the majority of the population. A generally peaceful Counter Reformation subsequently led by the Jesuit Order reconverted the nobility over the years, making Roman Catholicism basically the only religion of the Poles ever since.

In Przemyśl, one could also find remnants of the Polish-Lithuanian Commonwealth's Uniate Church, former Eastern Orthodox Christians who were brought under the Catholic pope in Rome following the 16th Century unification of Poland and Lithuania[47]. In modern times, the successors to the Uniate Church were known as "Greek Catholics". They were typically of Ukrainian ethnicity and mostly lost beyond Poland's borders due to territorial adjustments following World War Two. Nevertheless, a few remaining Greek Catholic church buildings – though many now in the hands of the Latin-Rite Catholic Church – offered a bit of variety to southeastern Poland's religious architecture, usually sporting rounded or onion-shaped domes. Sadly, ethnic tensions between Poles and Ukrainians in the early 20th Century left behind lingering contempt, and it seemed local Latin-Rite Catholics were sometimes still inclined to view these reminders of the Eastern Catholic presence as something foreign and not entirely welcome[48].

Despite the 16th Century union of Catholic and Eastern Orthodox Churches in Poland, Eastern Orthodoxy still had a noteworthy presence in the country. While Poland lay under foreign rule in the 19th Century, the Eastern Orthodox Church gained renewed patronage within the Russian Partition of Poland. Though most adherents were of Belarusian ethnicity and found themselves outside Poland after the post-war boarder changes, modern Poland's Eastern Orthodox Church still had over 500,000 members mostly in northeasterly provinces[49]. It was thus the country's second largest religious denomination, far exceeding the number of Protestants.

Eastern Orthodox church of St. Mary Magdalene in Warsaw

Tales from the PRL

Talking with my fiancée and her family, I was curious about what life was like in the old days under communism – particularly being an American who grew up on the other side of the Iron Curtain. I was familiar with the major historical turning points, but her family could tell me more about life for the average Pole, providing a more personal perspective on those times. The stories from my fiancée's childhood contrasted starkly with mine growing up in middle class America. We weren't especially well off, but still we lived in a large, amply furnished, single family home with a private yard and a porch with a barbecue grill. Our refrigerator and pantry were always stocked, my parents owned a big American luxury car, and I had a room full of toys, games, and books – and in the early 1990s even a personal computer.

When my fiancée was a child in 1980s communist Poland, people didn't have so much. Fewer people owned cars. Consumer goods were less varied and more difficult to obtain. Clothes were often ill-fitting as the correct sizes weren't always available, and she even remembered having to wear boys' underwear from time to time.

Children's toys were generally limited. She curses the communists to this day whenever she sees plush teddy bears. She remembered her bear being hard as a rock, stuffed solid probably with hay. Even as a grown woman, her eyes light up at the sight of aisles of fancy Christmas decorations which weren't so easy to come by in the 1980s. Around the holidays I'm torn between trying to restrain her in department stores and watching with glee as she indulges herself in ways she couldn't during her childhood. Our Christmas trees thus strain under the load of all the bling born by their heavily laden branches.

Like children anywhere else, of course, she certainly found ways to have fun in those days. She remembered making a dollhouse from a shoebox and even lighting it with a Christmas tree light which her dad rigged to a battery. She would play with other children in the green spaces between the big apartment blocks, and her parents didn't have to worry too much about her safety. In those days, most of the people who lived in their cluster of apartment buildings were from a similar demographic – young, married couples with children. The problems with roaming hooligans common in more recent times in such high rise residential neighborhoods wasn't so much an issue back then.

Her memories were of a rather gray world, though –

the gray of unpainted concrete buildings everywhere and those ubiquitous paving tiles forming the sidewalks. The two paint colors that did seem to be readily available were apparently standard issue mustard yellow and lime green. As a result, she abhors these colors even today.

She complained of a lack of taste in the food back then. Genuine chocolate was rare. Instead, children were likely to receive a "chocolate-like substitute" which resembled real chocolate and even tasted a bit like it, but was something artificial. As far as I was concerned, that alone would have been reason enough to overthrow the communist system. A more intensive taste came from flavored vitamins – *Vibovit* and *Visolvit* – in a powdered form meant to be mixed with water. As they produced a less-than-palatable-tasting beverage, children instead ate the vitamin powder like candy direct from the packets since these were the most exciting tastes readily available. Her favorite desert when growing up was *kogel mogel* – raw egg yolks with sugar and cocoa powder. The very thought of it made my stomach turn, but apparently it was a welcome treat.

I was a little dazed one day when she came out of the kitchen with a bowl of sugar-covered noodles in warm milk. *Zupa mleczna* (milk soup) I believe was the designation. She assured me it was an alternative to corn flakes during her childhood, as something seemingly so ordinary as breakfast cereal was not a regular part of the communist menu.

Meat was rationed, and she remembered mostly pork items and frankfurter type links (also lacking in much taste). The meat content of the average frankfurter was problematic. The issue was not that they contained a low content of meat, but whether or not there was actually any meat in them at all. With meat in short supply, the Polish diet included a lot of items which could be made from flour and potatoes like *pierogi*, crepes, and potato dumplings called *kopytka*. Cheese and seasonal fruits provided a little flavor and variety. For some reason, fresh oranges were a December tradition.

My fiancée was quite young when the communist system was overturned, and most of her childhood memories were from the transitional years of the 1990s. One of the biggest changes for her was how it suddenly became okay to want something. If she wanted a new item of clothing – a stylish t-shirt or a pair of nice jeans – this was no longer considered to somehow be wrong thinking. Consumer goods came flooding into Poland as the country's economy opened to the Western World, and only then did her parents get a color television. As we looked through her family photographs, I remember being surprised to see that most of her childhood photos up to 1990 were black-and-white. By comparison, I don't think any photos from my childhood were uncolored, and only one of our multiple televisions – an older unit we had in the kitchen – was an old black-and-white set.

The West, too, opened to Poland. When the transition from communism was marked by a period of high unemployment, my fiancée's mother traveled to work in the United States for a time. Upon her return with some foreign currency in hand, the family packed into their *Maluch* – an inexpensive but cramped little car produced in communist Poland – and took a drive to the south of France. It took about three days to get there and the car broke down repeatedly. Though they didn't have the money at that point to stay in a nice hotel or eat in the local restaurants, they were free to see the rest of the world without first needing authorization from their own government to leave the country.

A classic Polish Fiat or "Maluch" displayed in excellent condition at the Tyskie Brewery museum

While my fiancée was a child in the twilight years of communism, her parents and grandparents had seen it all. The Stalinist era following World War Two was the harshest, with the most intensive controls and propaganda, when everyone with a dissenting opinion was seen as a potential enemy of the state – from the heroes of the World War Two resistance, to Catholic clerics, to social democrats whose concept of democratic socialism was incompatible with totalitarian communism[50]. The older generations had to learn Russian, including reading the Cyrillic alphabet. My fiancée's father was still able to translate the label on a box we found housing an old

Russian slide projector. Her mother recalled being given an assignment in school to write about the sadness of the death of Soviet leader Joseph Stalin.

Surviving communist period statues at the Socialist Realism Museum in Kozlowka - (left) President Boleslaw Bierut, Stalin's leading Polish henchman, and (right) Russian communism's founding architect, Vladimir Lenin

With the end of the Stalinist period in the 1950s, communism's most fanatical years in Eastern Europe may have come to a close, but it was still only the beginning of a long struggle to keep the masses satisfied with this problematical socioeconomic ideology. In the latter decades, the large Polish community in the United States proved an important link to a more normal world for some in the old country, and ties between Poles in America and those back home helped to strengthen the positive image of the United States in Polish culture. Poles who had family abroad would occasionally receive care packages with everything from blue jeans and children's toys to hard currency. My fiancée's aunt even described being excited to get a box of scented laundry soap from America. She actually kept the box around after it was empty just to occasionally "smell the West".

In communist Poland, American dollars – though forbidden – became a popular currency due to their relative stability compared to the Polish *złoty*. My fiancée's parents explained that if someone worked in the States or received money from family overseas, technically he had to go to the bank and exchange his US dollars either into Polish *złoty* or into *bon towarowy*. These "*bony*", as they were colloquially known, were legal banknotes authorized by the Polish government which, in theory, held the value of the American dollar. In reality, real US dollars could get you more. With the communist government trying to maintain an artificial exchange rate for US dollars, there was a thriving black market in currency changing where people could purchase the more valuable American money.

Having US dollars made it easier to get an apartment, for example. Ordinarily, obtaining an apartment meant being on a long waiting list until something was available. Someone looking to move out from his parents' apartment, or a couple hoping for a larger place so they could start a family, might have to wait years. People could open a savings account with the government for their child, putting the child on the waiting list earlier in life, but my fiancée's mother was on a waiting list from childhood and she jokes even today that she is still waiting for the apartment they promised her. Ultimately her father managed to buy an apartment for her directly using American dollars.

In the 1970s, the government set up shops called *Pewex* (peh-vex) dealing exclusively in foreign currency, offering *bony* holders access to highly desired foreign goods – at greatly inflated prices. The communist government was heavily indebted to the West in those days, and needed all the hard currency it could accumulate. Thus it also made sense to sell even basic foodstuffs and household goods – items already in short supply – in the *Pewex* shops. But as time went by, it became more and more difficult to deny the artificially absurd state of affairs under communism.

The ongoing shortages were a recurring theme among Poles I've asked to describe those times. More than one Pole suggested to me that much of what was produced by the country's already inefficient, centrally directed industry was probably being sent to Russia. Getting the materials to finish an apartment wasn't easy. In those days, people couldn't simply go to a store and expect to buy what they needed for a particular job – even if money wasn't a problem. People often had to barter with workers at different construction sites and even resorted to "finding" materials on their own. In other words, borrowing from public projects without permission.

Since under communism everything was supposed to belong to the people, why not just sneak a few bricks from the public construction site down the street? As one story goes, when caught "sharing" the bricks from one construction project, a couple of eager young apartment owners were caught by a security guard. He asked why they didn't simply ask if they could take some bricks. They responded by inquiring if they still could, and the guard let them go their way with their newfound building materials.

The communist government's logic was simple – shortages existed not due to any deficiencies in communist economics, but because people were obviously consuming too much. Polish citizens were thus issued little ration cards called *kartki* which had tear-off coupons for an individual's or family's allotment of everything from food to clothing to gasoline. Meat rations were particularly prized and varied by occupation. Laborers doing physical work received the largest meat ration. Government personnel received a lesser meat ration but still more than the average citizen. Apparently the strenuous mental expenditures of bureaucrats required more protein intake. Everyone else got an even lower, standard ration.

Clothing coupons were for a limited time, which posed a problem when a needed item or size was out of stock – another routine frustration. My fiancée's father remembered having to settle for a pair of shoes that didn't fit in the hopes of selling them or trading with someone else who had a size closer to what he needed. It was better to have a pair of shoes that didn't fit than to have an expired ration coupon. Her uncle recalled walking into a store, noting the conspicuous emptiness of the shelves, and instead of wasting time asking if any of the things he needed were available, he simply inquired, "Is there something?" The storekeeper replied equally directly, "No, there's nothing."

Trading ration coupons or rationed items among friends, neighbors, or coworkers was common practice. A person might trade a chocolate (or chocolate-like product) coupon for an alcohol ration, a pork item for beef, or several items for an extra ration of gasoline if he wanted to cover any significant distance. That's assuming he actually had a car. It could take years to save up enough money to buy a car – new or used – and there was a waiting list for cars not unlike for apartments. Old films from those days showed a fair number of automobiles in big cities, but looking at period photos with my fiancée's parents, the streets of small towns were often practically empty except for the occasional "*ogórek*" – the Polish word for "pickle" applied to a roundish passenger bus made in the PRL.

Given the perpetual lacks of things basic to daily life and the sense of frustration and helplessness which stemmed from being little more than a statistic shuffled along by the mechanical processes of the system, often the only way to get ahead was to operate outside that system. A parent might provide "gifts" to curry the favor of the headmaster at a school, attempting to insure one's child went on to university and not hard labor. A shoe store worker might set aside some properly fitting inventory for the butcher so there would still be meat behind the counter when he arrived at the butcher's shop. Success had to be measured by even the smallest individualistic victories.

The only way to have more than your standard allotment – the only way to feel slightly in control of your own destiny – was to grab for more when no one was looking, to find a back door, to play the game better than your neighbors, your coworkers, your friends. Being patient and polite could cost you your only chance at getting what you needed. Everyone around you was a competitor who might cut ahead of you in some line and seize the last item on some shelf. There was no authority to turn to since the authorities *were* the system, its perpetuators and greatest beneficiaries. It was safest to simply keep quiet and fend for yourself.

As I considered the mindsets which developed among ordinary people just trying to get by in those days, the behaviors of some even in modern Poland made a bit more sense. People's attitudes toward civil society and authorities – and sometimes even the attitudes of authorities toward the people – still seemed burdened by the remnants of cultural mentalities ingrained during the communist years. Even examples of petty theft (and sometimes not so petty) from public places, right down to the stealing of toilet paper from public bathrooms, were problems that Poles were talking about many years after the end of communism. Obviously, one couldn't expect the effects of decades spent living under such conditions to immediately wear off.

I don't mean to sound entirely cynical about those times. The Poles did the best they could with an irrational societal model forced on them by Soviet Russia and Polish communism's cadre of local facilitators. While it was obviously easy for those within the party to give in to the overwhelming temptations of a corrupt system of unchecked power and privilege, others just as obviously thought the underlying goals of socialism were just, and wanted to believe the flaws within their government would eventually be fixed[51]. Some resigned their party membership when the Solidarity movement was met with the brutal imposition of Martial Law, events which made it clear the regime was not on the side of Polish workers. In the end, the 1989 Round Table Talks between communist party leadership and Solidarity led to a peaceful transition of power, and former communists who evolved into more respectable social democrats in the 1990s even got themselves democratically elected in the post-communist years.

The notion that the communists somehow escaped justice during the transition of power still irks some in Poland, though denying former communists the right to participate in a democratic society would have been a rather hypocritical ending to the story of the Poles' struggle for a free country. If they could, the far right today would probably still eject anyone from positions of authority who had links to the former regime. Yet attempts at "vetting" people in post-communist Poland for indications of collaboration with the communist secret police came to look like a McCarthyist witch hunt, in cases impacting innocent Poles who'd had little choice but to cooperate with the authorities under the old system[52]. Meanwhile the now social-democratic left has tried to remind Poles of communism's softer years around the early 1970s when populist reforms were attempted under First Secretary Edward Gierek to create a more "people friendly" version of communism[53]. This is all fairly recent history, and it will doubtless continue to be an occasional source of division within Polish society for some years.

Chapter Seven
Polish Politics – Right, Left, Center-cynical, and the Bigger Picture

For some of my fiancée's family members, politics was another taboo conversation topic at the top of the agenda. It's a subject I find fascinating but have to count among the dark arts. My perspective as an American on the events surrounding the end of the Cold War was the first thing to come up, which was something I was happier to discuss than contemporary domestic affairs. Specifically, I was asked about my thoughts on former US President Ronald Reagan, who I remembered positively for accelerating the end of the superpower standoff. I was still a child in the late 1980s and I don't think I understood much about politics then, but some years later I recall appreciating the power of Reagan's memorable speech before the Berlin Wall, a symbol of Europe's East-West divide, calling on Soviet leader Mikhail Gorbachev to, "tear down this wall."

Reagan is remembered among Poles for his strong stance against the Soviet Union and the communist regime in Poland. He voiced clearly America's solidarity with the Polish people manifesting their demands as he put it, "for freedom and dignity," while Poland endured the conditions of Martial Law in the early 1980s. Ironically though, while Reagan boldly encouraged the Solidarity trade union in Poland, his own Republican Party wasn't exactly known for being friendly to the unions in the United States.

Domestic politics

Following the end of communist rule, the Republic

of Poland's law was based on the Polish constitution of 1997 which organized the functioning of government and outlined the rights of the individual citizen. The legislature consisted of two houses, the 100-member Senate and the larger, 460-member house called the *Sejm* (pronounced "saym"). There was a directly elected president who served as head of state and chief of the armed forces, and an appointed premier (prime minister) who led the council of ministers (the heads of the various governmental divisions).[54]

While I'd rather not go into the details of Polish politics, I suppose it's an important component of any overview of the country, and it does seem like it's all they talk about on the news here. Poland has a democratic tradition which could be said to date back hundreds of years to the "nobles' democracy" of the Polish-Lithuanian Commonwealth and even earlier, though the tradition of democratic discord in Poland is equally well established. Poland today is of course a very stable country with governing institutions that transition smoothly from one election to the next, yet often intensive divides characterize Polish politics and Polish society on an ongoing basis.

Poland was sometimes described in the context of "Poland A" and "Poland B". Sometimes this was viewed as a political divide, sometimes an economic divide, sometimes a social or cultural divide. Broadly speaking, Poland A included generally westerly and better developed urban areas where unemployment was lower and living standards higher, with a majority inclined toward pro-European, moderate conservative, or socially liberal sentiments. Poland B would be categorized by less developed, often rural areas and small towns typically favoring ultra-conservative or nationalistic politics. Poland B was most commonly associated with eastern and even central parts of the country, with larger urban areas being something of a mix of perspectives. Perpetuating the notion of such divisions probably isn't helpful, but it's a concept most Poles are familiar with.

I've sat through an Easter Sunday mass with my fiancée's family where the priest was promoting literature suggesting which political orientations were appropriate for Catholic voters. I've watched as flag waiving nationalist groups marched through the streets championing everything from xenophobia to homophobia as examples of proper Polishness. The internet forums were particularly candid, where I've read in the comments sections of news web sites or YouTube videos angry accusations that particular Polish politicians were beholden to "Jewish" or otherwise foreign interests. Meanwhile social progressives proclaimed enlightened messages of tolerance and coexistence, yet with their sometimes bluntly anti-clerical bent showed little sensitivity to the deeply valued beliefs of the large Catholic demographic. In their defense though, it's hard not to understand the left's frustration with the unwavering devotion on the right when, for example, Poland's archbishop appeared to blame instances of pedophilia among the priesthood on society abandoning traditional values[55]. In the end, all the polarizing, emotionally exhausting rhetoric only drives the common people deeper and deeper into irreconcilable factions which can no longer work together to better the society around them. To the average American, such conflicting worldviews are all too familiar, in Poland simply flavored by a different national history.

Like many European countries, Poland had a parliamentary system of government with a political spectrum divided into multiple camps. No single political party generally gained an outright majority following elections. Instead, governance was accomplished by coalitions of two or more parties which could agree to cooperate on a particular agenda of legislative issues and to allocate governmental posts among themselves.

Numerous parties have come and gone in Poland since the end of communism, and breakaway parties still emerge every few years. This was one of the more obvious differences in Polish politics when compared to the United States, where the Democratic Party and the Republican Party have remained the only major political parties for about a century and a half. In America, party heads usually changed with the presidential election cycle, bringing with them a sense of renewal, a change of management to better align a party's strategic agenda with changing national circumstances. In Poland one could see the same political leaders at the heads of their respective parties even after failed bids in the national elections, with the parties very much defined by specific leader figures and the loyalty they inspired among a given voting bloc. Perhaps in this context, party members breaking off to form their own political groupings makes a little more sense.

I wouldn't be the first commentator to point out that Polish political parties at times seemed to represent something of a collage of political perspectives which might elsewhere be more clearly separated into rightist or leftist approaches[56]. For example, the otherwise rightwing Law and Justice party has been a proponent of government intervention to establish domestic control over certain industries[57], as well as more progressive income taxes[58] – protectionist and populist appeals more in line with leftwing economic strategies. Similarly, the reputedly pro-market Civic Platform was determined to nationalize the privately managed component of the state pension fund to plug a hole in the government's budget[59]. Meanwhile ex-communists in the center-left Democratic Left Alliance touted the victory of free market economics over the central planning of the old socialist model[60]. As I suggested at the beginning of this book, Poles have a knack for doing things their own way. Their mixed approach to traditional political orientations was no exception.

The center-right Civic Platform governed the country for an extended period beginning in 2007, and viewed close cooperation with the European Union as key to Poland's development. They seemed to have everything going for them as the country maintained economic growth even through the recent European recession, but lately, rising unemployment, slow wage growth, and controversial reforms to labor and pension laws have coincided with growing public discontent[61]. Socially, Civic Platform's diverse composition left it divided over attempts to pass legislation on sensitive issues like civil partnerships, abortion, and in vitro fertilization[62]. Civic Platform nevertheless provided a sense of stability in Poland for quite a few years, and succeeded in improving relations with the country's neighbors, repairing ties frayed during the preceding administration of Law and Justice[63].

The Law and Justice party maintained a steady appeal to the disenfranchised or otherwise dissatisfied, rallying its sizeable base with patriotic rhetoric and social values that attracted traditional conservatives. I really can't sugar coat this party much beyond such a generic description. Looking back, Law and Justice's administration from 2005 to 2007 divided the country over its focus on the influence of former communists in modern Poland, soured relations with neighboring Germany, and was beset by scandals related to the use of government security services for partisan political purposes[64]. More recently, Law and Justice's strategy seemed centered on fomenting conspiracy theories surrounding the crash of Poland's presidential aircraft in Smolensk, Russia in 2010, including insinuations that Moscow and Poland's Civic Platform government were both involved in some sort of cover up[65]. The quarreling between the Law and Justice party and Civic Platform has been a defining characteristic of the Polish political scene in the years that I've been here.

There were also other players on the field, all with a somewhat lesser following at the time. The Democratic Left Alliance was a center-left political grouping whose leadership emerged from Poland's former communist regime. In the new Poland, the old guard reformed themselves into a social-democratic party and successfully concluded Poland's accession to the European Union. Though the former communists proved relatively capable administrators in a free Poland, the Democratic Left Alliance lost control of the government in 2005 following high profile corruption scandals[66] which precipitated the electoral victory of the supposedly anti-corruption Law and Justice party. The Democratic Left Alliance has since continued to emphasize a traditional leftist message of greater social equality, while promoting a strongly pro-EU political platform including adoption of the European common currency and further EU integration.

Among the other, smaller parties was Your Movement (formerly Palikot), a fairly recent development which excited those eager for a more socially liberal voice in politics. After gaining a number of seats in the parliament, this libertarian party proceeded to push for the removal of crosses from public buildings in Poland, the legalization of marijuana, and the promotion of a transgender member of parliament[67]. They filled a niche in the Polish political spectrum, but the specifics of their agenda rather limited their appeal in a relatively conservative country.

Somewhere in the middle, but with a socially conservative base, was the Polish People's Party, a political tradition unmatched in its historical endurance. The People's Party could trace its origins all the way back to the political awakening among the Polish peasantry in late 19th Century Galicia[68], and its modern incarnation still had a reputation for focusing on rural or agrarian interests. Since its rebirth in 1990, the Polish People's Party has joined coalition governments with both the Democratic Left Alliance and the right leaning Civic Platform, and to date the People's Party has spent more time in governing coalitions than any other party since the end of communism – albeit as a junior coalition partner. The Polish People's Party had an impressive historical legacy, but in recent years has kept itself busy fending off nepotism charges[69]. The People's Party's image seemed in need of more than just a superficial makeover to achieve broader appeal in a 21st Century Poland, lest it find itself increasingly redundant together with a shrinking farming demographic that it competed for with the much larger Law and Justice party.

When I told my family I had decided to stay in Poland, I received a peculiar series of questions which probably offer some insight into the thinking of a lot of Americans regarding Europe. Firstly, Americans know very little about European politics, and usually fill in the gaps with presumptions and stereotypes that fit their existing worldview. For example, voices on the American right in particular criticize the French as a matter of course while having no idea what a strong and wealthy country France is. I know, because I spent quite a few years in the conservative Republican camp myself.

With respect to Poland specifically, I was asked why I wasn't concerned about living in a "basically socialist country". The European reader should understand that the Republican Party in the United States has made the worship of *laissez-faire* economics something akin to a religious faith, and defined their party as the opponent of "big government" and the "socialist" tendencies of the opposing, left leaning Democratic Party. The rightwing among the Republicans, predictably popular for their anti-taxation message, has encouraged the idea that all social services paid for by the government – like healthcare for example – essentially constitute socialism, which they've further sensationalized to mean the last stop on the road to communism and the end of individual liberty.

I oversimplify here a little, but oversimplification has been a key feature of the political discussion in the United States of late. In comparison, European thinking – which in fact places great emphasis on the wellbeing of the individual – seemed inclined to perceive the American government as overly beholden to corporate and banking interests, while falling rather short in its responsibilities to the welfare of its people. I had to remind the person questioning my choice to move to Poland that the Poles lived under genuine communism for many decades, and soundly rejected it.

Poland today, like most European countries, aims to follow the principles of social market economics. This allows for the creativity and effectiveness of capitalism and market forces, while assuming a significant role for the state in preventing abuses and insuring the basic welfare of the people. In some countries this has worked better than in others, but the uninformed commentator in the United States viewing the economic problems in places like Greece or Spain automatically comes to the conclusion that the "socialist" European model was clearly doomed to failure from the start. Once again, such a view is all too superficial, ignoring the specific problems certain countries have faced, as well as the existence of other European countries that have fared at least as well as the United States in the wake of recent crises.

Having lived in Europe for a time and traveled around the continent, it ultimately seems to me that cultural attitudes, varying greatly from one European country to the next, have played the greatest role in the successes and failures within different societies. In highly functional countries like Germany and Austria, I thought the level of cooperation among labor unions, management, and government to achieve positive outcomes for all three entities was admirable, contrasting greatly with the confrontational atmosphere prevalent among these components of society in the United States. I'm most impressed by the even more evolved mentalities found within Nordic culture. The Danes, Norwegians, Swedes, and Finns tend to shun self-aggrandizement and abhor corruption, instead valuing egalitarianism and transparency while maintaining laudably high average living standards. Frankly, both Polish and American cultures can be counterproductively egotistical at times, and both could benefit from a more modest, Scandinavian sensibility.

My impression has been that Poles are naturally suspicious of the motives of politicians, while at the same time easily roused by political voices condemning any hardships brought by particular reforms to the interests of this or that group of people. Yet the Poles still expect the government to come up with solutions to their problems. Thus, while the end of communism in Poland meant rapid decentralization and privatization, the government has nevertheless continued to play a very active role in the functioning of the Polish economy since then. The Polish government has been working steadily to secure massive restructuring funds from the European Union and to encourage foreign companies to invest in Poland. Smaller towns and poorer provinces benefit respectively from the transfer of tax revenues from larger cities and better developed provinces. Warsaw even bucked the fiscal austerity trend in Europe during the recent financial crisis, increasing government spending and riding out the following years more smoothly than most other countries in the EU[70].

Equally though, from the more conservative American perspective, the Polish people should also give themselves due credit. Very much despite a cumbersome bureaucracy, perpetual political bickering in Warsaw, and public infrastructure still lacking even two decades after the transformation from communism, the entrepreneurial efforts of private citizens with high expectations have steadily advanced and diversified the Polish economy of the early 21st Century. What has been accomplished in Poland since 1989 is very much a tribute to the Polish people's individualistic creativity and determination to prosper.

The European Union and other 'relationships'

Poland joined the European Union in 2004, so by 2011 being attached to Western Europe was nothing new for the Poles. EU participation was a natural direction for Poland after 1989, and the country has certainly gleaned calculable benefits from membership. With the disintegration of the former Soviet Bloc, turning to the EU allowed Poland to refocus its industry on exporting goods to western markets, and brought EU investment and modernization funds to Poland to upgrade the country's outmoded, communist era industry and infrastructure. Placards indicating the application of EU funding could be found everywhere, from the installation of sophisticated medical equipment in Polish hospitals to the refurbishment of historical sites. Even my fiancée was a direct beneficiary of EU grants available to women for training courses to improve their professional qualifications on the job market.

For better or for worse, many Poles have emigrated to Western Europe in search of employment opportunities in other EU countries. Similarly, university aged Poles I've met have traveled elsewhere in the European Union for seasonal jobs during their summer vacations, giving them a chance to earn higher wages and explore other parts of the continent. Not surprisingly, large communities of Polish migrants have decided to take up permanent residence in the United Kingdom, Germany, Ireland, and other EU states as continuing frustrations back home left Poland less appealing to its expats than the societies they found when they moved west. On the downside, this means that Poland itself has lost valuable talent which it didn't have a place for.

Poland had not yet adopted the European common currency – the euro – when I arrived. Skepticism of the monetary union was understandably high among the Poles. The difficult fiscal crises in progress in several euro zone countries made the prospect for Poland switching from its national currency less appealing. Talk of a euro referendum or adoption date was repeatedly pushed back even by the pro-EU Civic Platform government as the Poles waited to see if other euro zone states could overcome their ongoing financial struggles[71].

I've listened as some in Poland have decried, perhaps justly at times, that being a part of the European Union meant giving up too much control over the country's national sovereignty and submitting to rules of membership which, from one perspective or another, might not seem to be in Poland's best interests. No doubt lobbyists working in the EU's administrative capital of Brussels have indeed achieved the passage of EU-wide legislation which sometimes mandated conditions favorable to business interests in their own home countries. The Poles will tell you that property prices started rising dramatically after Poland joined the EU, with wealthy British investors quickly rushing in to buy up entire blocks of apartments, making it impossible for someone earning an average Polish salary to purchase a residence for himself. Supposedly the Germans did the same thing in places like Poland's Masurian Lake District, an area popular among Germans whose ancestors had lived there before World War Two.

Not all of the EU funding invested in Poland has been allocated without controversy, and the placards listing the EU contribution to a given project typically amounted to about half the total cost of the project. The rest of the subsidy was often covered by local debts which municipalities might take on simply to avoid losing the chance at the EU money. In theory, such debts should encourage investments in enterprises which will later generate enough revenue to allow for the repayment of those debts. However, upon hearing about the funding of airports and water parks in places where there wasn't enough demand to make them self-sustaining[72], I couldn't help but remember reading about the missed opportunities during the communist years to make economically justifiable investments with past financing from the West.

In the early 1970s, Poland borrowed large sums of money in the hopes of modernizing the economy, but in the end saw mainly short term rises in living standards thanks largely to the massive infusion of cash into the country[73].

Ultimately, though, blaming EU membership or the EU itself for various problems seems a little too convenient, diverting attention from addressing complex, national level issues like the competitiveness of businesses or the efficiency of government spending. In reality, rejecting EU membership would have excluded Poland from the region's biggest economic and political decision-making framework. European Union membership also obviously accelerated the adoption of Western standards in Poland. Countries like Belarus and Ukraine remained outside the EU in the decades following the breakup of the Soviet Union, and have progressed far more slowly than Poland both economically and politically. While Transparency International only gave Poland an intermediate ranking on its Corruption Perceptions Index, corruption levels were markedly higher among Poland's eastern neighbors beyond the European Union[74]. As for the British buying up properties here in Poland, I'm sure people from Britain who also complain about Poles emigrating to the United Kingdom to take British jobs would say it's only fair that the British be allowed reciprocal economic opportunities in Poland.

I understand that some in Europe fear the loss of national identities, but I doubt the Frenchman will ever stop being a Frenchman, or the German a German. The Poles' uncommon struggle to preserve their national identity during the Partitions should leave them particularly confident that they can continue to hold on to their sense of Polishness even while embracing a shared European identity. Continued EU integration and adoption of the best among Western European practices and standards should only raise the quality of life for the majority of Poles in the long run. Yet despite the EU's deepening integration, voter turnout for European elections has gradually fallen since 1979, reaching a low of 43% across the EU in 2009[75]. As I watched the evening news in Poland, typically half the broadcasting seemed to be about politics in Warsaw, while there was comparatively little coverage of the European Parliament or European institutions. Hopefully this will change in 2014 – an election year for the European Parliament – as the European Union will only be as representative and accountable as its people make it to be.

Within the European Union, Poland was part of a sub-set of member states known as the Visegrad Group. This was comprised of Poland, the Czech Republic, Slovakia, and Hungary – all of which shared a similar geopolitical and historical position within the broader European context, and perhaps more similar interests than those of westerly or southerly European countries. In post-communist Europe, cooperation among this group was originally aimed at joint EU accession, and since achieving that goal the Visegrad forum has continued through recurring meetings of the four countries' leaders, promoting cultural, educational, scientific, and defense-related ties[76].

Amidst ongoing participation within Europe, Poland has retained close, extra-regional ties with the United States. Polish sentiments about America have traditionally been very favorable. From the mass migration period in the 19th Century to escapees from the communist regime, America has been a place to which Poles throughout history have looked for opportunity and hope – my ancestors included. Polish-Americans sympathetic toward the struggles underway back in the old country provided support physically and financially at the most critical hours, lobbying for Polish independence during World War One, taking up arms in large numbers to fight against Poland's enemies, and supporting the World War Two Polish Government in Exile even after the conclusion of the war prevented it from returning to Warsaw[77].

Apparently, some high ranking figures in Soviet Russia suspected the election of the Polish-born Pope John Paul II was somehow engineered by the Polish-American national security strategist Zbigniew Brzeziński – though there's supposedly no evidence to support such a theory[78]. Brzeziński did, nevertheless, encourage America's Cold War strategy to draw Soviet satellite states in Eastern Europe away from the Soviet Union, and did have direct conversations with the Polish pope in the wake of his election. US sanctions against the PRL during the communist authorities' anti-Solidarity crackdown, together with President Reagan's stern warnings to Moscow not to intervene in Poland's internal affairs, made it clear the Poles' democratic aspirations had American support[79].

As the Cold War came to a close, with West and East German reunification raising concerns about old boarder settlements, American diplomats pushed for treaty language insuring that the Germans accepted the existing Polish-German frontier, discouraging claims to formerly German territories transferred to Poland at the end of the Second World War[80]. US trade with Poland accelerated with the normalization of the Polish economy, and the US government welcomed Poland's membership in NATO – the North Atlantic Treaty Organization – cementing Poland into the Euro-American defensive sphere. Poland, in turn, made noteworthy contributions to the wars in Afghanistan and Iraq[81]. Members of Poland's elite Special

Forces unit GROM have trained and fought side by side in combat with the renowned US Navy SEALs[82]. Military cooperation with the United States has also included technology transfers, including Poland's purchase of dozens of late model F-16 fighter-bombers as the Polish Air Force gradually phases out old Soviet military equipment[83].

That's not to suggest the relationship has been flawless. The aforementioned issue of visa requirements for Poles wanting to visit the United States has been a long running insult to a European people with such uncommonly positive attitudes toward America. When Bush-era agreements to install US anti-missile defenses in Poland were scaled back by the Obama administration, Washington had to assure Warsaw the changes were not made to appease well known Russian objections to the original plans[84]. Numerous errant references – made even at the level of the president of the United States – to "Polish concentration camps" or "Polish death camps" when speaking of facilities left behind in Poland by the Nazis have been a source of contention for Poles shocked by the careless use of language[85]. While referring to camps like Auschwitz as "Polish" due to their geographical location might seem inconsequential to Americans, the fact that the wording implies Polish responsibility is a serious affront to a people who suffered so much at the hands of the Nazis. Such diplomatic bungling doesn't seem to have had a terribly negative effect on broader Polish opinions, but no ally likes to be taken for granted.

In comparison though, despite positive Russian public opinion of Poland in the wake of the post-communist transformation[86], Warsaw's relations with Moscow have run into some definite rough patches. In part this can be seen as a result of Poland's self extraction from the Russian sphere of influence and eager partnership with the United States and European Union – in particular Poland's willingness to host American anti-missile defenses which the Kremlin treated as a direct challenge. In part this can also be blamed on difficulties with reconciling the darker pages in the history of Polish-Russian relations, like the Katyń Massacre, which the Poles became free to discuss after the passing of the communist order. The Poles have long seen dependence on Russian natural gas supplies as a potential strategic weakness, though these concerns should become less of an issue as Poland coordinates its bargaining position with the European Union and expands it import channels.

There were encouraging signs of progress following Poland's transition from the hard-line Law and Justice administration to the more tactful Civic Platform, together with the outpouring of Russian condolences after the plane crash which killed Poland's President Lech Kaczyński, but the diplomatic wrangling has continued to ebb and flow[87]. While the idea of American missiles stationed in Poland certainly provoked the Russians, Russian military exercises off the Polish coast in 2009 and high level references to Poland as a potential target for a nuclear attack were certainly excessive responses from Moscow[88]. I therefore found it comforting to know that an agreement was signed in 2011 for a regular US military presence on Polish soil[89]. I remember watching on the Polish news as the first units of a long term US Air Force contingent arrived. Witnessing the US-Poland alliance has been a bit surreal for me at times, like images of a US Air Force band playing American marching songs at a Polish Independence Day wreath laying ceremony in Warsaw. As an American living in Poland, to me such symbols of solidarity were really very moving.

Chapter Eight
A Government-approved Wedding

The visit to Przemyśl with my fiancée gave us the chance to take a look at a potential wedding site in the area – Krasiczyn (krah-shee-chin) Castle. We thought it might be a fitting continuation of our many "castle dates" and my proposal in Kraków's royal castle. It was all like something out of a fairytale, so we decided to stick with that theme. Krasiczyn was a gleaming white fortification comprised of cylindrical corner towers and walls rimmed with pointed spires. The surrounding park area was crisscrossed by little trails winding through the trees and around tranquil ponds, offering an enchanting backdrop for wedding photography. The castle was not far from Przemyśl, and my fiancée had been there many times as a child when in the area to see her relatives. For us it was a romantic setting close to her family, and an attractive destination for my relatives – some of whom had never travelled outside North America.

The picturesque Krasiczyn Castle, site of our wedding in June, 2012

Krasiczyn Castle was built in the late 16th Century by the Krasicki family as a defensive stronghold. Its fanciful renaissance style came later when an Italian architect was hired to give the castle a more palatial facade. The facility, now under government management, has since become available for public use, including comfortable hotel rooms and a dining hall decked with medieval armaments. The restaurant staff was equipped to prepare a formal dinner reception, and the castle's events planner handily managed all the onsite preparations. All that was needed was official permission to get married.

Who could have known that an American trying to marry a Polish woman could be such a complicated affair? I was about to endure the first of many experiences trying to get from point A to point B with the daunting Polish bureaucracy in between. In the old days under communism, the public bureaucracy existed to implement controlling rules and procedures covering every aspect of people's lives in order to insure the individual's total submission to the all-encompassing state[90]. Unfortunately, I'd have to say that many government offices dealt with by the average Pole today were still more oriented toward control rather than service. Even when government clerks I've encountered have clearly wanted to be helpful, they were frustratingly constrained by the complex nature of the processes they had to adhere to. At least one clerk inclined to talk offered us his sympathies for all the hoops they were required to make people jump through.

Our marriage application had to be processed through the Kraków court since my fiancée and I were both registered as residing in Kraków. The court had a duty to insure that we were not already married to other people, although the court itself didn't really do the checking. Rather, we had to go to our respective records offices and acquire the necessary documents to prove to the court that we were not otherwise wed.

Assumed guilty until proven innocent, this was a particularly difficult requirement for me since no such proof was required in the United States. To get married in my home state of Michigan, a person was simply required to sign an oath that he or she was not married. If it later turned out that the applicant had lied, the marriage could be annulled. I thus had to go looking for a document which I wasn't even sure existed. Fortunately, after a lot of searching I discovered that my state had begun providing a "certificate of no marriage" specifically for cases of Michigan residents getting married in foreign countries where this requirement existed. I suppose we were lucky it didn't occur to the court in Kraków to have me travel to the other 49 US States where I might also have been married.

I remember submitting our marriage application to the appropriate Polish clerk in person. The standard courthouse application form generally had a lot of options, and I got the impression from my fiancée that in any given situation it wasn't exactly clear what information needed to be filled in. Naturally, pens and pencils were not present with the stack of application forms. Asking to borrow one of the clerk's pens met with no success even though she clearly had several available on her desk. To be frank, the attitude of the average receiving clerk wasn't very supportive. If an applicant failed to know what he or she needed to fill out or attach with an application, this was not the clerk's problem. There was a separate office on another floor for asking questions. Several days later we would receive a registered letter from the court saying we had to come back and submit a second copy of our written request, a requirement which evidently the receiving clerk didn't know about or didn't care to inform us of. Little things like this just give people the impression the system really isn't there to help them.

I was shocked to see the big stacks of paper files being carted up and down the corridors of the court building. Everything seemed to be filed and stored on paper. Every application required an original copy of all supporting documents even if the court had already received such documents with a previous application. Perhaps this was because it was impossible to find the previously submitted documents in whatever massive records room was hidden in the sublevels of the building. There were computers in some rooms, which gave me hope that a transition was in progress toward at least a 20th Century electronic archiving system. However, these computers sat alongside the lady whose job was to sew together – using a gigantic needle and thread – stacks of documents so big that they could only be carried by those wheeled carts.

Shuffling people around from office to office looked to be a standard operating procedure. An original birth certificate was required for official applications like a marriage petition. While in the United States a person verified his identity with government clerks simply by showing a driver's license or state identification card, in Poland one had to purchase a new birth certificate and submit it together with such official applications as proof of identity. This meant making another trip to another government office nowhere near the courthouse. Purchasing several birth certificates at once to keep a few handy for future needs didn't work since applications required that a birth certificate be dated not more than 6 months old. Perhaps this was in case an applicant decided to change his birth date from time to time, or died recently and hadn't realized it himself. In reality, I think the underlying purpose here was simply to keep all the clerks employed whose job was to print birth certificates.

Months later I finally got to stand before a very sympathetic judge who only needed about five minutes to rule me fit to marry a Polish woman. Naturally, it was not enough to appear in court and ask a judge to issue an official ruling. At the eleventh hour, we learned that in order to get a physical copy of the ruling (needed by another office – the marriage office), we had to go back to the court yet again and file yet another application to receive an actual paper statement of what we had originally applied for.

I shudder to think just how many working hours have been lost by the citizens of Poland taking time off during business hours to run around the courts and various public offices filing one application after the next to advance their matters from clerk to clerk. Coming from the United States where a wedding could be accomplished in one fast-paced evening in Las Vegas, I could never have expected that the official approval to get married in Poland would be such a lengthy undertaking.

By the time we finally received the paper in mid-May saying we had permission to get married, it would have already been too late to get married in Kraków. For some reason, the process of submitting all the documents for the marriage had to be concluded at least one month before the wedding date. Officially, it was possible to shorten the 1-month waiting time with a written request, but according to the clerk in the Kraków marriage office, it was the policy of the office to ignore such requests. She could give us no reason for this official disregard for the official policy. The only conclusion I could reach was that the purpose of the various government offices we dealt with was not actually to facilitate any particular process, but instead to find any possible excuse to deny an official permission. It was lucky we were getting married in a small village in the east where the officials were a little more accommodating.

Finally, on a warm and slightly overcast morning in June, my fiancée and I were married on the garden steps of Krasiczyn Castle in a very official ceremony amidst family and friends from all around the world. We'd gone with a civil ceremony since I wasn't Catholic, and Protestant wedding ceremonies in Poland didn't result in a legal marriage certificate. The local civil clerk stood before us in a dark suit, with a silver chain around his neck bearing the image of the Polish Eagle. The proceedings concluded with the signing of the Act of Marriage document in a fancy, red leather folder suitable for a grand international treaty.

Wedding rings in Poland were generally worn on the right hand, whereas in the United States they were worn on the left. As a side note, we later thought we'd spotted a trend among certain affluent individuals in Warsaw to break with the Eastern tradition and wear their wedding rings on the left hand.

At the end of the wedding ceremony, my wife's family surprised me with the Polish tradition of tossing handfuls of coins at us – which we had to collect from the stone walkway to insure future financial security. We then adjourned to a toast on one of the castle's balconies, and later enjoyed a sumptuous dinner in the main hall. Introductions on both sides of the family had been accomplished with both my wife and I translating here and there. Her parents also spoke English, which proved quite helpful. Her grandfather had learned that if he spoke Polish slowly and loudly, I could understand most of what he was saying (by then I had spent a year studying the language). I was afraid he may have gotten the impression that the rest of my family would be equally capable of basic communication. Alas, it turned out English was not a distantly related, slowly spoken dialect of Polish, but everyone seemed to be all smiles nonetheless.

I've been told traditional Polish wedding celebrations could include several days of drinking and feasting, but we went with a more American style finish that evening, concluding with the cutting of the wedding cake after dinner. One custom I'm told was common at Polish weddings was having plenty of food to take away afterwards. If there wasn't a pile of leftover meats and breads and cakes, the hosts must have gone cheap. Fortunately, the castle's staff had prepared so much extra food that we had to carry it out on a hand cart suitable for service hauling documents around the Kraków courthouse. After all the months of preparation and stress, we couldn't have been happier.

Chapter Nine
Making Poland Home

Our bureaucratic hurdles were not over, of course. The next step for me as a foreigner was to get permission to reside in Poland. After marrying a Polish citizen, I could still only apply for a 1-year permit initially. Following that period I could apply for another 2-years, and then finally permanent residence. After a year of permanent residence, I could even apply for Polish citizenship.

Thankfully, the residence application was a relatively simple process and took about a month in total. My wife and I sat through brief interviews in separate rooms at the provincial government building, ensuring we could answer the same basic questions about the relationship and that the wedding wasn't some kind of sham marriage by two people who didn't actually know each other. The next week, I received a positive response and picked up my *karta pobytu* – my Polish identification card.

My wife initially faced more post-marital hurdles than I did. For her to adopt my surname she had to pay for a new identification card, driver's license, and a plethora of applications at the court and various government offices to update official records related to her property in Kraków. Updating one's official government identification card (*dowód osobisty*) apparently did nothing to inform other government bureaus of official changes in a citizen's personal details. This lack of automated communication between branches of the bureaucracy made marriage significantly more complicated and costly for a woman than for a man.

Women had more red tape to deal with in the United

States as well following marriage, but the processes were simpler. In America, one had to register name changes at the Secretary of State office for one's state as well as at the Social Security Administration for the federal government. I believe this pretty much updated all the other government databases. Driver's licenses, which doubled as official identification in America, could be changed at the Secretary of State office on the same visit, sometimes even via the same clerk.

Life among the concrete towers

At first, my wife and I lived in her apartment in one of those standardized, communist period housing blocks ubiquitous in Poland. Similar structures could be found throughout the former Eastern Bloc. Their contemporaries in Western Europe and North America usually constituted low income public housing projects. In communist Poland these were built in several basic formats over the years to meet the expanding housing needs of average citizens. Ours was of the twelve storey variety, built fairly solidly from preformed concrete panels, though finished to a questionable standard in many respects.

Finding straight lines in the building was a challenge, particularly when trying to hang a picture. There was a danger of electrocution when drilling into the walls since the location of wiring between electrical outlets was often difficult to predict. To save on wire in the old days and probably sell any "extra" materials on the black market, builders often connected wires as directly as possible, leaving them strung diagonally behind the walls or otherwise randomly strewn. The little lavatories in the middle of the apartments echoed terribly, and our upstairs neighbors' bath sloshed around so loudly we were certain their overgrown Christmas carp was still swimming laps back and forth in the tub. There must have been something perpetually wrong with the water pump, as the water pressure from our taps on the eighth floor dropped to a slow trickle on multiple occasions throughout the year.

In the old apartment buildings, the living room often doubled as the master bedroom for a couple who had children. The couch folded out into a bed, and the door to the living room could be closed to give the parents some privacy at night. In the States we described an apartment by the number of bedrooms it had. Thus an apartment with two bedrooms and a living room was referred to as a two-bedroom apartment. In Poland, an apartment was referred to by the *total* number of rooms it had. Thus an apartment with two bedrooms and a living room was a three-room apartment, perhaps emphasizing that there were three rooms which could potentially be used for sleeping. Space was at a premium, and from time to time when my wife and I tried cooking together in the narrow little kitchen, I likened it to working in a submarine.

Since the economic transformation of the 1990s, individuals and building administrations have been remodeling these old apartments to bring them up to a higher standard – sometimes even as nice as in more recently built apartment blocks. The exteriors of the buildings were wrapped in insulation and usually painted in brighter colors than the bare, concrete gray finish of the communist days. Windows, likewise, have gradually been replaced to further improve the buildings' energy efficiency. I remember a communal sense of excitement when our block's management finally exchanged our old, open elevator with one that had a door. On the downside, the sound of drilling into the concrete walls carried throughout our building on a regular basis – an irritating fact of life for residents as the renovations seemed endless. My wife and I wondered just how many more holes could be drilled into this giant house of concrete cards before the whole structure finally came crashing down.

There were other minor downsides to life among the concrete towers. Finding a parking space was a daily problem. Returning in the evening when everyone else was already home from work often meant parking on a street somewhere far from our apartment. The communists simply hadn't designed the parking lots with the expectation that every family would someday have one or more automobiles. It was common to find every official parking space taken, fire lanes practically impassable, and vehicles driven up onto any accessible patches of grass alongside the parking lots – grass which therefore turned to mud in the fall and spring.

Old ways of thinking died hard, and people repeatedly stole the light bulb hanging in front of our storage locker in the basement – probably to put it in front of their own locker where their bulb had burned out. Why waste valuable time and money buying a new light bulb when someone else had carelessly left a perfectly good one just hanging there in the socket a little farther down the corridor? If something was in a communal space, surely that meant it didn't belong to anyone.

My wife – being particularly ecologically conscious – also tried replacing the older, energy-intensive, incandescent light bulbs in the corridor in front of our apartment door. She exchanged them with energy saving fluorescent bulbs, but these too quickly disappeared when someone apparently noticed the more valuable lights available on our floor. This finally stopped, however, when she took a permanent marker and wrote on the plastic part of the bulb, *THIS LIGHT BULB WAS STOLEN FROM…*

and indicated our address.

The large cluster of big apartment towers in our area meant the neighborhood was densely populated. This was typical of Polish urban planning during the communist period since communism didn't exactly agree with the personal space and displays of individual success that went with suburban home ownership. After the communist system passed, income disparity widened, and suddenly very poor people lived in the same apartment buildings as the rising Polish middle class. Unfortunately, poverty brings with it challenges which are pretty much the same in any country, including heightened levels of low level public disorder and something of an apathetic disregard for public spaces. Our neighborhood often had problems with local hooligans roaming drunken through the green spaces between the blocks at night, singing, shouting, chanting football slogans, vandalizing the walls with graffiti, and occasionally setting fire to paper recycling bins because apparently it's fun to burn stuff.

In some buildings, people who'd lived in the big apartment blocks for most of their lives knew who their neighbors were, and together sort of kept an eye out for the troublemakers. Elsewhere, people I've heard from felt very isolated, surrounded by people who they didn't know and who they could see were involved in some of the problems they observed outside their windows. Police and city security patrols were scarce, evidently due to limited resources. At times I think the only sense of community in existence was a communal sense of frustration among the otherwise civil segment of the population.

In other matters, the Polish way of thinking continued to leave me scratching my head. For example, one day the national government tried to come up with a way to better cover the cost of household trash removal, together with instituting a countrywide recycling scheme. Various ideas were bounced back and forth around the halls of parliament and ran the gauntlet of the national news networks. Finally a plan was arrived at to have each household pay a fixed fee per current resident. The trouble was, when it was time for the Poles to report how many people resided in each household, half the population of Warsaw suddenly seemed to have disappeared. A similar phenomenon occurred in Kraków where the population of certain districts evidently dropped overnight by tens of thousands when the data from this voluntary census came in[91]. Apparently the reaction of the clever Pole was: why would someone report the presence of four residents in a particular dwelling if that meant paying four times more for trash removal?

In what was perhaps an overenthusiastic embrace of commercialism when communism ended, advertising agencies blanketed city streets with closely-spaced billboard and banner advertisements – the bigger and gaudier the imagery the better. In cases, entire buildings were hidden behind catchy slogans or images of bikini models whose scantily-clad breasts were blown up to the size of automobiles. With historic architecture vanishing behind giant advertisements, cities like Kraków had to ban such building-sized banners from the old town center, but dense clusters of billboard signs remained pervasive elsewhere. I'm sure my marketing professor from university would have said the effect of such advertising was minimal, since the intended messages were ultimately lost in all the marketing "noise".

Apparently the Polish government wasn't thrilled about the situation, and legal action was considered to limit such signage. As soon as this was suggested, however, the Polish advertising industry rallied to put a stop to it, claiming the legal restrictions would cause severe damage to the economy and a loss of employment for "thousands" of people – presumably the huge workforce employed in making billboards. On the other hand, with ten times more billboards in Warsaw than in Paris, it wasn't hard to make the case that the level of advertising clutter was detracting from the appearance of Polish cities.[92]

Personally, I would also suggest all the billboards and banners along the streets make it harder to spot traffic signs, which are already confusing enough in Poland. In principle I favor limited government interference in the affairs of private citizens and businesses, but as we say in the United States, with freedom comes responsibility.

That's certainly not to suggest the agents of the modern state themselves were always encouraging when people wanted to be good citizens. One day, a little old lady living in an apartment above one of the market squares in Kraków noticed the city's flower planters were empty. Apparently due to a lack of funds, the city wasn't planting anything around the square that year. The elderly lady, thinking she might be able to do something for the neighborhood, proceeded to sow some flowers in the planters. Once they started to grow, however, employees of the city's infrastructural management agency – ZIKiT – came along and started digging up the fresh sprouts. When she asked why they were culling the flowers, the city employees replied that they thought the sprouts were weeds – which apparently the city *did* have the money to deal with. As the old lady protested, explaining that the green shoots were indeed flowers planted in the vacant pots, the ZIKiT workers sent her away with a warning that she could be fined for tampering with city property. When the media got hold of the story, the administration at

ZIKiT assumed a more conciliatory tone, but on the lower level dealt with by the little old lady the official treatment was automatically controlling and reproachful.[93]

Of course, though it's easy to ridicule some aspects, those were certainly happy times for me and my newlywed wife. We were excited about our new life together, and I was getting used to the idea of settling down in Poland permanently. It wasn't a bad lifestyle in general. We had quick access to the city center by public tram, and even enjoyed bicycling all the way to the old town for lunch or a cup of coffee. There was a lot of green space planned around our group of apartment buildings from the 1980s, nicely counterbalancing the slightly stark style of the communist era construction and making it a decent place to go for an occasional walk. The day-to-day chores weren't too difficult with a supermarket and a couple of convenience stores within walking distance of our building – including a small cluster of shops ironically dubbed "Manhattan". We lived just a short drive from a large shopping mall as well. Perhaps the best feature of life in that high rise housing tower was the fact that our apartment was on the eighth floor and offered an impressive view over the city.

One happy little discovery here in Poland has been the celebration of "name days" – *imieniny* (ee-mee-eh-nee-nih) in Polish. One's name day is the calendar date associated with the Catholic saint whose given name a person bears (Saint Christopher, Saint John, Saint Paul, etc.), and traditionally in Poland name days were more likely to be celebrated than birthdays. I've thus come to enjoy two days devoted to me each year. Living in Poland, I receive gifts and good tidings on my name day from family and friends here; but being an American, I still celebrate my birthday and usually get presents in the mail and greetings via the internet on that day as well.

The Poles look forward to any occasion to celebrate something, and the Polish calendar is replete with special days. In the United States, mothers and grandmothers both celebrate Mothers' Day together. In Poland, however, there is one date for mothers and another date for grandmothers. The same holds true for fathers and grandfathers, who each get a separate day devoted to them. There's also a day devoted to women – International Women's Day on March 8th. Originally a socialist idea which was promoted during the communist times, the tradition remains a popular occasion to recognize the accomplishments of women and to lavish flowers and chocolates on them at their places of work. This is in addition to Valentine's Day on February 14th, a very American tradition which has recently gained popularity in Poland too. New Years Eve celebrations, called *Sylwester* in Polish, are a huge event, particularly in Kraków where the market square is packed on the night of December 31st with revelers present for concerts and midnight fireworks. Surprisingly, Saint Patrick's Day hasn't caught on yet. It seems like the perfect holiday for the Poles' love of celebration, mixing Catholic tradition with alcohol and festivity.

Building a house in Poland, a.k.a. more bureaucracy

Our long-term plan was to sell my wife's apartment and build a house on a plot of land she owned. I must assume the rules and regulations affecting homeowners in Poland were written with good intentions, but maddening little technocratic hurdles waited for us at every turn – including contradictory regulations. One rule said we had to build exactly in line with our neighbor's house, which rested about 2.5 meters from the city's land, while a new regulation indicated that homes had to be built at least 4 meters from the edge of city property. The burden was of course on us to obtain a waiver to overcome the conflict in the city's rules.

The original plans for our house were for a dwelling about 16 centimeters longer than our adjoining neighbors' house. The rules changed before we started building, and suddenly adjoining houses had to be the exact same length, forcing another amendment to our plans. To this day we're stuck with a garage slightly too short to comfortably open the rear hatch of our station wagon while parked inside. We were lucky our neighbors hadn't built a 3-meter-long shack, presumably limiting us to building an equally small dwelling.

We ran into more problems later when it was time to build a driveway. The standard driveway width on a street the size of ours was apparently 3 meters, but we had already built (and had approved) a two-car garage, necessitating a wider driveway. This was ultimately unacceptable, however, as the people writing the rules related to driveways had not envisioned two-car garages, thus it was not possible to be granted permission to build such a driveway.

We faced seemingly endless running around filing separate applications to appease a plethora of overlapping government authorities with their many lengthy approvals processes. The volume of documents needed to get all the approvals was boggling. We had to submit to the city's architectural office literally armfuls of plans and copies of plans for the house itself, which was a perfectly ordinary private residence. Every page of every required copy had to be individually reviewed and stamped as approved. Just getting everything together to make the utilities connections required a stack of documents as thick as a brick.

ZIKiT – the same city bureau known for digging up flowers planted without permission by old ladies – apparently required homebuilders to provide a plan for moving heavy equipment to and from a residential building site so that a survey could be done of the neighborhood's streets. Once the construction was completed, another survey would be done to determine the wear and tear on those streets during that period. From what I understood, the homeowner was then responsible for any holes or deformations in the road surface which had since developed. It didn't matter if the damage was caused by the city's trash truck or snow plow or freezing and thawing in the spring or fall. It was assumed that the homeowner's construction equipment was responsible.

Having gotten lost among all the many requirements, one day we had a surprise visit by a ZIKiT patrol car as our cement truck arrived at the other end of the neighborhood. Yes, it seemed the infrastructure office had its own patrol cars just like the police. Instead of politely informing us that we needed to address our failure to apply for the advance street survey, the ZIKiT inspector drove into the driveway, parked so as to block the entrance to the construction site, leapt from his car, and started shouting at our builders that he was going to call the police to have us fined for not having followed ZIKiT's procedure. As with some other players in the realm of officialdom who we encountered, the ZIKiT official apparently felt what was most important was that he demonstrate his power to prevent things from happening.

In dealing with various public officials and offices, I began to understand why the Poles were so inclined to try to sneak around the official processes in order to get things done. Whether discussing private citizens or businesses hoping to operate in Poland, contradictory regulations and manifold, unpredictable, time consuming approvals couldn't help but slow down the pace of economic progress. We were, after all, employing a construction firm and a small army of workers and craftsmen, and buying all sorts of building materials and home appliances and furnishings. Building and finishing a private home is probably the biggest contribution the average individual makes to the economy outside his place of employment, and one would think that governmental administrations would want to maximize the individual's chances of succeeding in this endeavor rather than creating as many obstacles as possible to hinder the process.

Other inexplicable hurdles came in the form of seemingly simple things like ordering a telephone line. Apparently even in the 21st Century, it was still not possible to connect to the telephone network in some urban areas. Poland's landline telephone infrastructure belonged to Telekomunikacja Polska, essentially a monopoly descended from the former telephone service of the communist era and since taken over by Orange Polska, a private company. When we called to have our new house connected to the network, we received the blunt reply that no service was available at our location, and that extending service to our end of the neighborhood would require too much investment in infrastructure. It wasn't as if we lived in the countryside somewhere; we lived within the limits of the city of Kraków, the second largest city in Poland, and just a couple blocks in from a major avenue. What was most frustrating was that looking out our window, we could see the nearest telephone line was just across the street from us.

As we commenced the construction of our house, we

became privy to a litany of negative stereotypes that some people held about Polish construction contractors. People warned us of builders taking money up front and then not showing up for work, skimping on quality to pocket the savings, or stealing our purchased materials to resell them elsewhere. Contrary to this sometimes negative reputation, we had a very positive experience, hiring a single developer to handle the project from start to finish. They provided us with very professional service, laying out in our contract a timeline for completion, a fixed budget, and milestones at which payments were to be made for completed work. They fronted all the costs for materials needed before each scheduled payment, and dealt with most of the subcontracting on their own.

The typical Polish thinking seemed to be that by haggling with individual suppliers and negotiating with different contractors, the individual homeowner could get the better deal in the long run by going it alone. Surely hiring a developer would cost more because they wanted their own cut. In the end, trying to build a home bit-by-bit over time sourcing different contractors for different stages of the construction process could mean unpredictably escalating expenses and long delays based on workers' availabilities. Professional construction firms buying materials on a regular basis probably received better discounts from suppliers, and could provide that critical piece commonly missing from the Polish homebuilding puzzle – a well planned budget.

We did occasionally have to hire outside contractors for specific jobs, and only then did we get to meet the stereotypical runaway worker. We had to use an authorized electrician to install the outside circuit box which connected to the electrical company's network. The electrician did a fine job with the installation, but once he was paid, he failed to provide us with the certified documentation needed by the electrical company. After he failed to drop the document in our mailbox as promised, he stopped answering our repeated phone calls. Apparently recognizing our telephone number on his caller ID, he kept ignoring our calls until we tried contacting him from another number. This time he answered the phone immediately. He grudgingly agreed to meet us at a set time to deliver the document, but never showed up for the appointment.

Clearly, there were still those contractors who had a very poor concept of a work ethic. Once he had gotten his money, he had no interest in following through and completing the job. One can only hope that with reliable contractors competing on the Polish market like our main building team, the majority of the unscrupulous workers like that utility technician will be driven into another line of employment. Drastic though that may sound, Poland will be a better place to live when Poles can feel more confident about trusting each other.

I have to give most of the credit for the ultimate success of this project to my amazing wife. As my skills with the Polish language left much to be desired, she handily coordinated the most intricate details, on multiple occasions having to overcome the sexist preconceptions of certain small-minded vendors (again, not including our primary contractors). A chemist by trade, her more recent career experience in project management made her a natural team leader, and I'm proud to say she's my favorite example of what Polish women are capable of when they're determined to accomplish something.

The community

Living in the suburbs amidst the little streets of individual family houses made Poland feel much more like home than our time in the big, utilitarian housing blocks. Random little houses with neatly tended yards reminded me of life back in the small American towns where I'd spent most of my preceding years. People generally took better care of their own properties than the sometimes lackluster efforts put forward by the building administrations managing apartment blocks. The councilman from our city district and a number of volunteers were particularly active on behalf of the neighborhood, even organizing an annual picnic in the fall with a blazing campfire and live music from a small band of Highlanders dressed in traditional costumes. Such community spirit was a very natural part of small town life where I came from in America.

A sense of community can be a very powerful force for good; when people know their neighbors and interact with them in positive ways, they're more inclined to look out for each other, to concern themselves with each other's shared interests. When residents become organized and seek to manage matters in their own neighborhoods, it's a bottom up rather than a top down approach to how a society functions. Poles frequently complain about obvious community problems over tea or a bottle of vodka shared among friends, but often the impression I get is that the only force presumed capable of dealing with such problems is some governing authority, or that it's simply not worth trying to do anything because things will never change. The communist era notion that people should shut themselves into their homes and wait for whatever the government decides to do is really out of place in a democratic society.

Although our neighborhood was generally very pleasant and well kept thanks to the efforts of its residents, there were still areas where we thought a little community cooperation might make a big difference. Small patches of woods here and there were marred by deposits of household trash, and public properties often appeared overgrown and untended. The local shopping center was regularly vandalized with graffiti, and the shop owners apparently didn't see it as their responsibility to pick up the empty beer cans and broken bottles strewn around their steps.

Eager to support community initiatives in our little corner of Kraków, my wife and I joined in with the local picnics and did some occasional trash cleanup in the woods near our house. We also obtained a permit to do a little groundskeeping on the overgrown city land adjacent to our yard, property which the city simply didn't have the money to maintain. We wanted to try rousing more of this kind of local responsibility, so we thought we'd attempt to tackle the problem of vandals spraying graffiti on the walls of the nearby shopping center.

Roaming hoodlums would sit and drink in the park at night and then spray paint the walls of the closed shops on their way home – often with vulgar or racist images and slogans. We asked a few of the shop owners if they would be interested in volunteers from the community coming to help repaint the vandalized walls. They didn't seem particularly optimistic, having repeatedly dealt with this problem themselves only to have the walls sprayed again shortly thereafter. But they didn't want to turn us away. So we went to our local councilman and proposed the idea to him, suggesting we try to obtain donations of paint from around the neighborhood and to gather a small group of volunteers to help out with the physical work. His response was more enthusiastic, himself having led various neighborhood initiatives like the annual picnic.

My wife and I sat down with the councilman and hashed out a plan, together with a ranking officer from the *straż miejska* – the city security forces whose involvement would be necessary to better monitor the frequently targeted area. The official thinking – that of the *straż* – was a little disappointing though. The officer expressed frustration with the fact that the *straż* could only fine shop owners for not removing the more vulgar graffiti, and not just the ordinary variety. In other words, he seemed disappointed it wasn't easier to punish the victims. This official reaction helped us to understand the response of the shopkeepers who felt it was a waste of time to report such crimes to the authorities. With law enforcement personnel being such an important part of any community, it was an image which such services needed to improve. We were thus only further motivated to come to the aid of our neighbors.

Before long, we had a plan to spread the idea of our volunteer action through the councilman's media contacts and announcements in the local church. The priest said he'd try to get other parishes involved, and to include an anti-graffiti message in the religion classes for young people in area schools[94]. Soon enough we had national media coverage as we rolled our donated paint over the offensive graffiti outside the shops. The national police force was also starting to crack down[95] on graffiti crime around Kraków, which made us feel like we were doing our part to help out with a broader campaign to clean up our streets.

Obviously the graffiti problem was something that everybody recognized, and one which the city was officially trying to combat. From our perspective, the biggest hurdle seemed to be getting ordinary citizens to understand that even though it was someone else's shop or someone else's apartment building vandalized this time, it was in fact a problem affecting all of us and requiring a community response. It was also obvious that a small group of do-gooders would never be able to counter all the graffiti crime in Kraków. That really wasn't the point. Trying to keep the woods clean in our neighborhood had been an equally frustrating exercise, with people repeatedly returning to dump their bulky items like old computers or broken flooring tiles even after we put up signs indicating we were trying to keep the area clean. What was important was that we were trying to pull the community together to face these sorts of problems. Maybe the hooligans would keep spraying the walls of the local shops, but we – the community – would keep coming back too, refusing to submit ourselves to those within society who refused to behave themselves in a civilized fashion.

Ultimately our goal was to inspire others around the city to adopt the same approach, volunteering to deal with problems in their own neighborhoods. Waiting around for central authorities to fix things can be an exercise in futility because it presupposes that those authorities actually understand the problems people face. In the end, oftentimes it turns out that the most effective solutions to problems lie with those most directly involved – a fundamental principle in any democratically organized society.

Examples of civic activism have in fact been on the rise in Kraków as well as other Polish cities[96]. One recent example of an activist initiative that gained enough popular momentum to affect public policy was the

Krakowski Alarm Smogowy – the Kraków Smog Alert. Owing to Kraków's high smog levels, particularly in winter due to the burning of coal and, at times, trash by private residents, the Kraków Smog Alert raised public awareness and encouraged the switch to cleaner home heating systems. Naturally, convincing the broader public was not an easy task, given the high costs that would have to be incurred across thousands of individual households utilizing old coal burners. Eventually though, city management ended up banning the installation of coal and wood stoves in new home constructions within the city, and setting a target date several years down the road for the replacement of these heating systems in existing homes[97]. How exactly this would be implemented had yet to be worked out as of early 2014, and I worry the city will drag its feet and end up having to postpone the deadline when it arrives. But it looked like local government was eventually capable of understanding and acting on the will of citizens expecting specific issues to be addressed.

In the case of the efforts that my wife and I were involved in, we certainly weren't alone. Aside from our ambitious councilman, we teamed up with our next-door neighbors to deal with the trash problem around our block, and on a broader scale we were also volunteering with a couple small groups of university students who were already looking for opportunities to get involved in such positive civic activities. We've even had some luck trying to build a sense of community in the low income housing blocks nearby, encouraging people to come out for coffee and doughnuts to discuss their problems together. The more active we've become, the more we've come into contact with other Poles determined to organize private initiatives to bring about changes that benefit us all. Citizens' movements have been bringing attention to a variety of urban planning and development issues, from the management of downtown traffic to the preservation and maintenance of green spaces around the city. Meeting ordinary people passionate about improving the quality of life in Poland, and seeing the desire particularly among younger Poles to contribute, leaves me with a feeling of optimism for Poland's future.

Chapter Ten
More "Polish" Geography

From seaside resorts to mountain lakes

There are plenty of noted cities and sites in Poland which I haven't yet had the opportunity to mention in this text. There was the beautifully preserved old town of Zamość (zah-moshch) in the southeast, founded in 1580 as an ideal example of Renaissance period urban planning. There were the big château-like palaces of Książ (ksh-ohnzh) and Moszna (mosh-nah) in Silesia. There was the major seaport city of Szczecin (shcheh-cheen) in the northwest holding a certain attraction for a former mariner like myself. The centrally located city of Łódź – a quintessentially Polish spelling pronounced "woodge" – was one of the country's largest urban centers, and during the 19th Century Partitions was the leading center for textile production in the Russian Empire. My travels around the country continue, and I have yet to explore so much of what remains to be seen.

The colorful Renaissance town square in Zamosc

Traveling to the Baltic seaside was a traditional summer holiday for many Poles, though it was a long journey on a slow train or crowded roads for those of us from as far south as Kraków. Sopot was a small, coastal resort town known for its beaches and its long pedestrian pier – the longest wooden pier in Europe. Cool summers and cloudy weather on the Baltic Sea were frequent inhibitions to visiting beachgoers, but sunny days brought out large crowds. Determined Polish sunbathers could often be seen erecting personal windbreaks in the sand around their beach blankets to fend off frequently blustery conditions.

The beaches and pier at the Baltic resort town of Sopot

Sopot's bustling promenade leading in from the seaside was packed with open air cafés and restaurants. Bypassing the pricier establishments, we went straight for the good stuff and indulged in a sweet desert called *gofry* available from numerous sidewalk cafés. *Gofry* is a thick waffle topped with any number of sugary condiments like whipped cream, chocolate syrup, fruits, and jams. The best are served fresh and warm, dripping with melted chocolate. It's a messy summer treat best eaten over a sticky sidewalk already dirtied by everyone else nibbling at their heavily laden waffles.

Gdynia, the most northerly component of the coastal tri-city area (comprised of Gdynia, Sopot, and Gdańsk), was a relatively new settlement, dating from the time of the Second Republic. The town slowly grew around the seaport established there in the 1920s, and modern Gdynia included shipyards, Poland's naval headquarters, public beaches and piers, and – to my delight as a mariner – was home to a pair of Polish museum ships, the World War Two destroyer *Błyskawica* (Lightning) and the three-masted sailing ship *Dar Pomorza* (Gift of Pomerania). Gdynia's main pier was lined with eating establishments and pubs, many offering seafood caught locally on the Baltic. Fried flounder was a local specialty well-suited to topping off a morning spent exploring the pier-side attractions.

The museum ship Błyskawica, a Polish World War Two destroyer on display in Gdynia

Modern navy warships could also be seen making

port in Gdynia on occasion. These included the missile frigates *Generał Kościuszko* and *Generał Pułaski*. Both were transferred to Poland from the United States Navy following Poland's entry into NATO in 1999, and both were named for Polish military officers who fought in the American Revolution.

In winter, Poles were frequent visitors to the country's southern mountain ranges. Ski resorts and thermal spas could be found throughout, and every weekend the roads out of Kraków were jammed with people making the drive south. The mountains were often cloaked in a foggy overcast from all the coal stoves of the highland cities and towns. But when the skies cleared, a beautiful, snow covered landscape of rolling hills and black forests was revealed. I'm not much of a skier myself, but I certainly enjoyed soaking in the thermal baths. It was a surreal yet relaxing experience sitting in an outdoor swimming pool in the winter with snow falling on my head, yet being perfectly warm, heated by the hot, steamy water piped into the pools.

One of the most prominent ski destinations was the mountain town of Zakopane (zah-koh-pahn-eh). Lying in a valley below the High Tatra Mountains, the city was a base camp for exploring the highest peaks in Poland as well as a center of Góralski (Highlander) culture. There was no missing the Góralski cheeses and woolen clothing on offer at little outdoor vending stands, and traditional wooden architecture could be found throughout the area. During the warmer months, hiking along the mountain trails became a major attraction, and the trek to Morskie Oko – the Eye of the Sea – was a popular route not far from Zakopane. Morskie Oko was a large, roundish body of water pooled in a depression between the mountain slopes. The rocky gray rise of Mount Rysy, Poland's highest peak, towered above this dark blue lake surrounded by evergreens.

While America's most famous dam is the Hoover Dam, Poland's downscaled version is the Solina Dam in the southeastern corner of the country. It was located in the forested highlands of the Bieszczady (bee-esh-chah-dih) Mountains sandwiched between Slovakia and Ukraine. The Solina Dam was one of the more impressive infrastructural achievements of the communist period, completed in the late 1960s to prevent recurring flooding downstream as well as to take advantage of one of Poland's few potential sources of hydroelectric power.

From the home of my wife's grandparents in the city of Przemyśl, we followed the San River south and eventually wound our way up to Lake Solina, a large, artificial lake formed above the Solina Dam. After the dam was completed, Lake Solina quickly became a popular tourist destination, and on our visit my wife pointed out the old "sanatoriums" lining the hillsides. In Polish, a sanatorium was something like a spa prescribed by a doctor for people deemed in need of rest and recuperation. There were park areas and marinas, and scores of little sailboats tacked back and forth across the wider parts of the lake. Lacking our own sailing vessel, we took a leisurely motorboat tour on one of the little ferries which also putted around on a regular schedule.

Solina Dam (top) and sailing on Lake Solina (bottom)

About a hundred miles (around 160 kilometers) north of Przemyśl lay the city of Lublin, the biggest city in

Poland's eastern provinces. Lublin has played host to some very important moments in Polish history. It was the site of the Union of Lublin in 1569 which officially created the united Polish-Lithuanian state. Later, following 123 years under the foreign rule of the Partitions, Lublin was the location where the first domestic government was established upon the restoration of Poland's independence in 1918. Continuing the city's prominence in Polish history, the Polish Committee of National Liberation also got its start here in 1944, officially beginning Poland's period of communist rule. Although easterly cities like Lublin struggled economically in the post-communist years, being saddled with communist era industry and situated far from Western European export markets, Lublin was home to several universities, and its rather large student demographic was something that stood out to me. Its educational facilities included state institutions like the Maria Curie-Skłodowska University, as well as the John Paul II Catholic University of Lublin which offered studies not only in theology but also in the sciences – from a Catholic perspective.

In the northeast corner of the country lay the Masurian Lake District, a naturally beautiful region dotted with over 2,000 lakes. Like North America's Great Lakes region, Poland's Lake District was carved out by glacial activity before recorded history – though on a smaller scale. The largest lake was Śniardwy (shnee-ard-vih), which was maybe one-fifth the size of Lake Tahoe in California. Śniardwy and various other lakes in the district were popular destinations for recreational sailing and other water sports in the warmer months, and many of the lakes were connected by rivers and canals.

The area was heavily forested as well, featuring protected nature reserves. Following the forestlands past

Białystok toward the Belarusian border, the Białowieża (bee-ah-woh-vee-eh-zhah) Forest was a noteworthy national park area. These were primeval woodlands, examples of Europe's old growth forests. The Białowieża Forest was home to the continent's once nearly extinct stock of European Bison, called *żubr* in Polish. Though similar in appearance to the bison of North America, the European Bison was a forest-dwelling species while the American Bison was more common to the grasslands of the plains.

Nearby, Poland still shared a small stretch of border with Russian territory. To the north of the Masurian Lake District lay the Russian *oblast* of Kaliningrad. Kaliningrad was a coastal province located between Poland and Lithuania with a northwesterly shoreline on the Baltic Sea. Separated from the rest of Russia with no overland connections, it was a little Russian outpost wedged into the side of the European Union. For centuries the province belonged to the German state of Prussia, but at the end of World War Two most of the German population either fled the advance of the Soviet Army or was expelled shortly thereafter. The Russians later rebuilt their bombed-out portion of Prussia into a major Cold War military center.

Tensions around the province increased again in recent years with Russia's response to cooperation between Poland and the United States on anti-missile defenses. In protest – as a chilling reminder of Russia's strategic capabilities in Central Europe – the Russian military staged war games in the vicinity and deployed ballistic missiles to Kaliningrad[98]. The hostile rhetoric comes and goes, but given all the difficult history in the region and the importance of Russian natural gas supplies to Poland and other European Union countries – as well as to the Russian economy – it was really in everyone's best interests to get along.

On the edge of Eastern Europe

Travelling east beyond now easterly Polish cities like Suwałki, Białystok, and Przemyśl, east beyond modern Poland's borders, one arrives in lands which were long associated with the Poles but ultimately segregated when most of the Polish-speaking people there were driven westward at the end of World War Two. Poles today whose ancestors had to move west after the war can trace their roots back to cities, towns, and villages which now find themselves in foreign lands. Those former eastern lands, called the *Kresy* in Polish, became parts of modern Lithuania, Belarus, and Ukraine, but continue to hold a place in the Polish national memory.

In past times, the population of these eastern lands was ethnically mixed, and Polish speakers comprised large communities throughout – including people of other ethnic backgrounds who became "Polonized" linguistically and culturally over the centuries. Noted figures from throughout "Polish" history like the democratic revolutionary Thaddeus Kościuszko, the poet Adam Mickiewicz, and Marshal Józef Piłsudski had Lithuanian or Ruthenian roots stemming from the times when the concept of "Polishness" could be a social and political identity as much as an ethnic background. However, the majority of the people living in those lands were never a part of that largely aristocratic stratum, and the rise of ethnic nationalism in the latter 19th Century subsequently recast the cosmopolitan past in a negative light. Nationalists on all sides thus sought to claim the same territories as their own in the early 20th Century.

Following World War Two, with the Soviet Army

occupying Eastern Europe from Minsk to Berlin, the United States and Britain agreed with their wartime Russian allies to shift Poland's borders farther to the west, accepting hollow Soviet guarantees about free elections and democratic states. Few Americans today will remember President Franklin Roosevelt for his role in Eastern European ethnic cleansing. On the heels of the massive wartime deportations already perpetuated by the Soviet Union, the long-running regional ethnic disputes were settled by expelling around 1.5 million Poles from the midst of other nationality groups in the east and resettling them within Poland's redrawn borders. Around the same time, most of the remaining German speakers in Poland's western provinces were similarly driven even farther west, and ethnically-motivated butchery was taking place between Poles and Ukrainians in the vicinity of their new border.[99]

Fortunately the late 20th Century brought a degree of rapprochement to the region, particularly as the growing yearning for independence from Soviet-enforced communism was recognized as a cause common among Poland and its eastern neighbors. Importantly, this was the notion endorsed by the Solidarity movement in Poland. Polish policy finally evolved to support the national aims of Lithuania, Belarus, and Ukraine, and offered reassurances that Poland respected its existing eastern borders. Upon the collapse of the Soviet Union, Polish leaders chose a path of reconciliation and practical cooperation with their neighbors rather than rehashing divisive historical claims over the territory of the *Kresy*.[100]

Of course, it would be naïve to suggest that people on all sides were entirely devoid of nostalgia, or that entrenched prejudices have completely disappeared. The modern Polish-Lithuanian relationship has seen its ups and downs over Lithuania's restrictions on the linguistic rights of the remaining Polish minority there[101]. Meanwhile in Poland, instances of Lithuanian-language road signs being vandalized[102] or an anti-Lithuanian banner unfurled by hooligans at a soccer match[103] have revealed unfortunate sentiments still harbored by some Poles as well. In Kraków I met an ethnically Lithuanian student who grew up in northeastern Poland, in an area which was for centuries inhabited by both Poles and Lithuanians but in modern times found itself on the Polish side of the border. She described the local Poles as being "unfriendly" to the Lithuanian speakers in her village, and I suspect she was putting it mildly. At the very least, on an official level these two neighboring EU countries and fellow members of the NATO alliance speak in terms of having a strategic partnership[104], and educated young people, like my Lithuanian acquaintance, were able to see beyond the old differences.

The Polish minority in western Belarus has perhaps endured the greatest official hardships in recent years, having to contend with the authoritarian, anti-Western regime of President Alexander Lukashenka who viewed the Belarusian Polish minority with suspicion for the democratic and pro-Western elements among them[105]. When the Soviet Union disintegrated, some among Belarus' evolving political apparatus were interested in forming ties with Western European institutions, but these efforts were quickly stunted as President Lukashenka came to power[106]. His administration has since kept Belarus very close to Moscow's orbit, maintaining a level of military and economic integration with Russia reminiscent of Soviet times[107].

The city of Lwów (lvoov) was predominantly Polish and Jewish when it was attached to Poland after World

War One, but together with the surrounding area was then made a part of Ukraine at the end of World War Two. Called L'viv by Ukrainians, this historic city lay not far across the modern border from the southeastern part of Poland where much of my wife's family lived. At one point, my wife and I walked across the border on foot together with the regular lineup of people buying cheap cigarettes and alcohol in Ukraine for resale in Poland. Importing such items in large quantities was met with tariffs, but carrying limited amounts for "personal use" was allowed, creating a steady stream of cross-border foot traffic. "Ants" was how the local Poles referred to these busy little couriers.

On the Ukrainian side we caught a bus to L'viv which wound its way down a bumpy, two-lane road for a little over an hour, crossing the intervening countryside and passing little Ukrainian villages along the way. Some of the homes lining the roads were downright rustic while others were larger, modern homes built for wealthier Ukrainians in styles which would have easily suited their Polish contemporaries. The landscape was mostly indistinguishable from what we'd left on the Polish side of the border. The driver, however, displayed his Byzantine-style icon of the Virgin Mary and Christ Child next to the Ukrainian flag above his seat, and peppy Ukrainian folk music poured from the speakers for the duration of the journey. Together with the Cyrillic text everywhere and the golden-domed, Greek Catholic churches dotting the hills and valleys, there was no forgetting that this was Ukraine.

L'viv's historic city center appeared in pristine condition around the time of the Euro 2012 soccer championship co-hosted that year by Ukraine. The region's shared heritage with southern Poland was evident in much of the downtown architecture. The 19th Century styling paralleled that of Polish cities like Kraków and Przemyśl, which – together with L'viv – were all part of the Austro-Hungarian Empire's province of Galicia during the Partitions. The visitor to L'viv in the early 21st Century found still more layers of history built atop old Lwów. Following World War Two, new districts were added, and large, standardized apartment blocks from the communist years furthered the similarities with cities on the Polish side of the border.

Ukrainian food shared much in common with Polish cooking, including *pierogi*, cabbage, and breaded pork cutlets. The Lychakiv Cemetery with its many monuments and fanciful mausoleums was filled with the graves of Poles lying side by side with Ukrainians – though sadly many of the Polish grave markers had been defaced or destroyed at some point. The Russian language was compulsory in Ukraine during the Soviet period and could be found on street signs together with Ukrainian. We were surprised, however, to find English writing had also been added to the signs in L'viv's city center to better aid the many international tourists.

The familiar look of L'viv's older streets (top), and L'viv University, the former Galician parliament building (bottom)

Little did we know at the time of our visit, but Ukraine was on the verge of a major crisis that would again alter the course of history for this long contested land. Unlike Poland, Ukraine was formerly a constituent state of the Soviet Union, and eastern and southern Ukrainian provinces were populated by a large number of Russian speakers. Much of Ukraine's industry was located in the east, closer to Russian markets which consumed about a third[108] of Ukraine's exports. In contrast, much of western Ukraine was long oriented toward Western Europe, an integral part of the Polish-Lithuanian Commonwealth when Ruthenian noblemen were among the most powerful magnates in old Poland, and later lying outside the Russian Empire as a part of Austro-Hungary in the 19th Century.

After gaining independence from the Soviet Union in 1991, Ukraine found itself torn between closer ties with the European Union or with Russia. Ukraine's Yanukovych government calling off work on an association agreement with the European Union in late 2013, under the threat of economic reprisals from Russia, intensified the underlying divisions. Pro-Western Ukrainians – particularly young Ukrainians – saw EU integration as the means to building a more normal country and bringing positive changes to a corrupt political and economic oligarchy[109]. Civil unrest ensued leading to the fall of the Russian-leaning administration, but events took an even more drastic turn when Russian forces seized control over parts of Ukraine, threatening to tear the country apart.

Regardless of the outcome of this ongoing regional drama, Ukrainians led the inflow of Eastern European migrant workers into Poland[110] just as Poles were migrating even farther west for similar reasons. I came to know a number of Ukrainian students during the course of my Polish language classes in Kraków. Poland was a window to the west for its eastern neighbors, and a model to be studied. I would say it is Poland's ongoing mission, the mission of the Polish people, to be such an example, the success story, the hope for what is still possible in the East of Europe. The triumph of liberty.

Closing Remarks

The Poles observed a multitude of official holidays which offered a day off from work, many of which were traditionally religious in nature. Perhaps the most appropriate to mention in closing this text would be All Saints' Day. On November 1st, sidewalk vendors set up stands selling flowers and little memorial candles, and people made their way to crowded cemeteries to offer their prayers and remembrance for the departed. The tradition was Catholic and the faithful were obliged to observe mass on this day, but even non Catholics made appearances at the graves to pay their respects to loved ones who had passed.

Parking, as usual, often became a difficult affair, and steady streams of people could be seen flowing up and down the streets near the cemeteries and along the narrow little paths between the rows of tombs. By the evening, the graveyards were flickering fields of candlelight shimmering through multicolored glass jars, called *znicze* (znee-cheh), set before the headstones. Arrayed in flowers and burning candles, the graveyards took on an almost warm, almost inviting atmosphere even on a chilly, rainy autumn day.

It wasn't difficult to feel reflective in such an environment – to remember not only those who had passed, but to look back upon life in general and on all the people and events that had brought me to where I was. I remembered my father, who we'd lost to cancer just a year before I made my first trip to Poland. My grandfather died when I was very young, and I could only imagine what the rest of my Polish ancestors were like. As I lit a candle in remembrance of family members long since departed –

setting it before cross erected for those whose graves were not present in the Kraków cemetery – I felt as though I'd reached some sort of epiphany, that I'd succeeded somehow in tying us all together.

Genealogical research has proven a popular hobby in the United States. Diversifying culture in America and the open discourse on the country's changing demographics have sent Americans like myself searching to rediscover their unique origins – to place themselves and their present circumstances into greater perspective, to better understand their role in the American and broader human story. I suppose I took that search to the extreme by actually returning to live in the land of my ancestors. For many years after the fall of the First Republic, those ancestors still called themselves Polish even though no such country as Poland existed. With respect to my own Polish heritage, my experiences in Poland have brought me to the conclusion that what was lost for a time – as with Poland itself – was never truly lost.

After the restoration of Polish statehood in 1918, some Polish-Americans indeed returned to Poland but often found themselves out of place. According to Polish-American historian John Bukowczyk, Poles back in the old country who'd endured the hardships of the Partitions and the First World War weren't particularly welcoming of those who had emigrated and then returned with their own ambitions for Polish society[111]. The factional struggles within Polish democracy and the authoritarian regime of the Piłsudski years left other émigrés who might have returned to Poland very grateful for the life they had in the United States.

My own experiences in modern Poland have reminded me of just how American I am, coming with a different perspective to many things I've encountered –

though the world I found in Poland was often more familiar than foreign. Naturally, there are some things I miss about life in the United States, not the least of which is the rest of my now very distant family. So much of the American lifestyle is about making things more convenient and user friendly. Americans love and expect happy endings, which I think becomes something of a self-fulfilling prophecy in contrast with traditional Polish skepticism. Yet despite occasional frustrations, Poland is a pretty exceptional place as I hope this book has helped to reinforce.

Personally, I hope to have many long and happy years here. I look forward to eventually cultivating my backyard garden like so many of my Polish neighbors, to playing with my dog on the lawn, to exploring more of Poland's many intriguing historical sites, and to recurring hours spent chatting with friends at outdoor cafés in Kraków's bustling old town. I've even become an avid tea drinker, and learned to eat my sandwiches without a second slice of bread on top. One little irony I'll just have to live with is that when my Polish ancestors changed our surname from Błażejczyk to Bloswick to make life easier in America, they never considered the difficulty Poles would have spelling the name Bloswick while I was living in Poland. *"Błosłyk?"* *"Blos-veetsk?"* Blah.

Selected Bibliography

Applebaum, Anne. *Iron curtain, the crushing of Eastern Europe*. New York: Penguin Group, 2012.

Bukowczyk, John. *A history of the Polish Americans*. New Brunswick: Transaction Printing, 2009.

Davies, Norman. *Heart of Europe, the past in Poland's present*. Oxford: Oxford University Press, 2001.

Snyder, Timothy. *The reconstruction of nations*. New Haven & London: Yale University Press, 2003.

Storozynski, Alex. *The peasant prince*. New York: St. Martin's Press, 2009.

Zamoyski, Adam. *Poland, a history*. London: Harper Press, 2009.

Endnotes

[1] Snyder, Timothy. *The reconstruction of nations*. Chapters 1 and 6.

[2] Davies, Norman. *Heart of Europe, the past in Poland's present*. p. 261.

[3] Davies, pp. 259-260.

[4] Zamoyski, Adam. *Poland, a history*. Chapters 9-11, also pp. 207-217.

[5] Bukowczyk, John. *A history of the Polish Americans*. p. 14.

[6] Premier.gov.pl. 6 November 2012. *Gas prices for Poland over 10% lower*.

[7] Evans-Pritchard, Ambrose. The Telegraph. 21 August 2013. *Poland's shale drive will transform Europe, if it does not drop the ball*.

[8] European Commission, Directorate-General for Economic and Financial Affairs. April 2013. *Member states' energy dependence: an indicator-based assessment* (occasional papers 145).

[9] Zamoyski, pp. 404-405.

[10] Główny Urząd Statystyczny. *Bezrobocie. Stopa bezrobocia*. Accessed 2 December 2013.

[11] Central Intelligence Agency. *The World Fact Book*. Poland. Accessed 15 July 2013.

[12] Ewing, Jack. The New York Times. 22 December 2013. *Midsize cities in Poland develop as service hubs for outsourcing industry*.

[13] Monaghan, Angela. The Telegraph. 3 October 2007. *Cadbury to move jobs to Poland*. Also The New York Times. 8 January 2009. *Dell shifting production to Poland from Ireland*. Also Pope, Stephen. Flyingmag.com. 17 May 2012. *Eclipse jet production moves to Poland*. Also Ciferri, Luca. Automotive News. 11 February 2013. *Fiat to move 500 output from Mexico to Poland, sources say*. Also Leggett, Theo. BBC News. 19 September 2013. *Why Germans are moving to Poland to do business*. etc. etc.

[14] Worldbank.org. Poland Overview. Accessed 2 October 2013.

[15] Eisenbrey, Ross and Gordon, Colin. Economic Policy Institute. 6 June 2012. *As unions decline, inequality rises*.

[16] OECD.StatExtracts. Labour – Trade union density. Accessed 25 January 2014.

[17] Ibid., Central Intelligence Agency.

[18] Rosenthal, Elizabeth. The New York Times. 4 April 2008. *Old ways, new pain for farms in Poland*.

[19] Zamoyski, pp. 289-292.

[20] Applebaum, Anne. *Iron curtain, the crushing of Eastern Europe*. pp. 332-346.

[21] Dempsey, Judy. The New York Times. 1 September 2010. *In Poland, a memorial becomes a battleground*.

[22] Crestodina, Thomas. Krakow Post. 19 January 2011. *Krakow Police hold five for machete killing*.

[23] BBC News. 11 November 2012. *Poland Independence Day march turns violent.*
[24] Goettig, Marcin and Florkiewicz, Pawel. Reuters. 11 November 2013. *Far-right rioters leave trail of destruction in Polish capital.*
[25] Ibid., *Bezrobocie. Stopa bezrobocia.*
[26] TVN24.pl. 11 November 2008. *Patriotyzm to sprzątanie podwórka i płacenie podatków.* Also Tokfm.pl. Portal Opinii. 11 November 2012. *Nowoczesny patriotyzm jest społecznie zaangażowany.*
[27] Storozynski, Alex. *The peasant prince.*
[28] See Taylor, A. J. P. *The Habsburg Monarchy, 1809-1918.* Bloomsbury: Hamish Hamilton, 1948.
[29] Zamoyski, pp 267-268.
[30] TVN24.pl. 18 June 2013. *Pendolino bez pendolino, czyli włoski pociąg na polskich torach.*
[31] Storozynski, p. 10.
[32] Zamoyski, Chapter 20. See also the Home Army Museum in Kraków and the Warsaw Rising Museum in Warsaw.
[33] Applebaum, pp. 49, 72-76, and 209-219.
[34] <www.zamekbobolice.pl> Accessed 23 August 2013.
[35] Piechowiak, Łukasz. Bankier.pl. 24 March 2011. *Dlaczego paliwo w Polsce jest drogie.*
[36] US Energy Information Center, eia.gov. 1 May 2013. *State gasoline taxes average 23.5 cents per gallon but vary widely.*
[37] Gazda, Sylwia. TVP.pl. 19 December 2012. Budowa S3 coraz bliżej.
[38] Gazeta.pl. 16 July 2013. *W Polsce autostrady buduje się drożej niż w Niemczech. ETO krytykuje marnotrawstwo unijnych pieniędzy.*
[39] Devictor, Xavier. The World Bank. 14 June 2012. *Poland: aging and the economy.*
[40] Adams Sheets, Connor. International Business Times. 29 September 2012. *The East European Miracle: How did Poland avoid the global recession?*
[41] Ministry of Treasury, Republic of Poland. 29 April 2013. *Support for corporate R&D in Poland – state of play and challenges.*
[42] Piątkowska, Marta. Gazeta Wyborcza. 25 April 2013. *Za dużo młodych studiuje, zamiast zdobywać zawód. Co trzeci bezrobotny nie skończył 25 lat.*
[43] Zamoyski, Chapter 1.
[44] Warsaw Business Journal. 17 May 2012. *Polish health system one of the worst in Europe: report.*
[45] Główny Urząd Statystyczny. *Wyznania religijne stowarzyszenia narodowościowe i etniczne w Polsce 2009-2011.*
[46] Ibid.
[47] Snyder, Chapter 6.
[48] Ibid., pp. 211-212.
[49] Ibid., *Wyznania religijne stowarzyszenia narodowościowe i etniczne w Polsce*

2009-2011.
[50] Applebaum, p. 266.
[51] For example, Kapuściński. See Domosławski, Artur. *Ryszard Kapuściński, a Life.* London & New York: Verso, 2012.
[52] Harris, Emily. NPR News. 19 October 2007. *Communist-era scars haunt Poland's politics.*
[53] Wprost. 2 January 2013. *SLD: niech rok 2013 będzie rokiem Gierka.*
[54] The Constitution of the Republic of Poland of 2nd April 1997. <www.sejm.gov.pl> Accessed 26 October 2013.
[55] Thenews.pl. 17 October 2013. *Top archbishop blames child abuse on 'pornography, divorce and feminism'.*
[56] Zamoyski, p. 398. Also en.poland.gov.pl. Political parties. Accessed 8 December 2013. Also Wójcikowski, Rafał. Money.pl. 19 January 2004. *Plan Hausnera wisi na związkowym włosku.* Also The Economist. 1 October 2012. *Polish protests.*
[57] Newsweek Polska. 8 December 2012. *Kaczyński: konieczna repolonizacja mediów I banków.*
[58] Dziennik.pl. 6 April 2013. *Kaczyński chce docisnąć bogatych podatkami.*
[59] Forbes. 7 October 2013. *Poland's piggish pols – they're not alone.*
[60] Boniecka, Ewa. Warsaw Business Journal. 11 July 2011. *Leszek Miller, a view from the left.*
[61] Sobczyk, Marcin and Wasilewski, Patryk. The Wall Street Journal. 11 September 2013. *Polish protestors demand new government.*
[62] Fakt.pl. 28 January 2013. *Głosowanie nad projektami o związkach partnerskich wygrał Jarosław Gowin.*
[63] Day, Matthew. The Telegraph. 7 October 2011. *Polish government to become first to be re-elected since fall of communism.*
[64] Easton, Adam. BBC News. 22 October 2007. *Analysis: Poles tire of twins.*
[65] Rzeczpospolita. 19 September 2013. *Macierewicz: Sami wyznaczymy ekspertów do debaty.* Rzeczpospolita. 20 September 2013. *"Eksperci Macierewicza nie są specjalistami od katastrof lotniczych".* Warsaw Business Journal. 23 September 2013. *Smolensk experts controversy.* Gazeta Wyborcza. 23 October 2013. *Kaczyński w "Gazecie Polskiej": "Moskwa naciska, by zakończyć sprawę Smoleńska".*
[66] Repa, Jan. BBC News. 1 April 2003. *Poland gripped by 'bribery' row.*
[67] Gera, Vanessa. The Huffington Post. 20 January 2012. *Poland's Janusz Palikot tries to smoke pot in parliament.*
[68] History from the party web site: <www.psl.org.pl/historia/>
[69] Wprost. 8 August 2008. *Pawlak nie przyjmuje zarzutów o nepotyzm.* Also Gazeta.pl. 12 March 2009. *Pawlak: Zarzuty "Dziennika" to insynuacje.* Also Polskie Radio Dla Zagranicy. 23 July 2012. *Agricultural corruption case opened.*
[70] Adomanis, Mark. Forbes. 10 January 2013. *If austerity is so awesome why hasn't Poland tried it?* Also M. C. K. The Economist. 18 December 2012. *Don't*

forget Poland.

[71] Stratfor Global Intelligence. 10 July 2013. *Poland shies away from euro zone accession again.*

[72] Czarno na Białym. TVN24.pl. 22 March 2013. *Totalny odlot* and *Popłyną na aquaparkach?*

[73] Davies, pp. 367-370.

[74] Transparency International. *Corruption Perceptions Index 2012.*

[75] Europa.eu. European Parliament. *Turnout at the European elections (1979-2009).* Accessed 22 November 2013.

[76] <www.visegradgroup.eu> Accessed 11 December 2013.

[77] Bukowczyk, John. pp. 49-50 and 87-92.

[78] Vaughan, Patrick and Gati, Charles. *Zbig – the strategy and statecraft of Zbigniew Brzezinski.* Baltimore: The Johns Hopkins University Press, 2013. pp. 127-128.

[79] Zamoyski, pp. 374-377.

[80] Snyder, pp. 235-236.

[81] CNN. 22 November 2001. *Polish forces to join Afghan campaign.* Also 7 May 2003. *Poland helps to rebuild Iraq.*

[82] TVN24.pl. 19 April 2013. GROM ramię w ramię z SEALs.

[83] Wilk, Andrzej. Ośrodek Studiów Wschodnich. 23 October 2013. Holes in the skies over NATO's Central European member states.

[84] The Associated Press. 18 March 2013. *US reassures Poland over missile defense changes.*

[85] Storozynski, Alex. The Huffington Post. 29 November 2010. *The Wall Street Journal understands history, when will the rest of the American media?.* Also Landler, Mark. The New York Times. 30 May 2012. *Polish premier denounces Obama for referring to a "Polish death camp".*

[86] Snyder, pp. 278-279.

[87] Levy, Clifford. The New York Times. 17 April 2010. *Russia and Poland: a blood feud rooted deeply in the past.* Also The Warsaw Voice. 18 December 2012. *Russia vows to return presidential plane wreck, Polish media skeptical.*

[88] Brunnstrom, David. Reuters. 18 November 2009. *NATO critical of Russian wargames near Poland.* Also McElroy, Damien. The Telegraph. 15 August 2008. *Russian general says Poland a nuclear target.*

[89] Office of the Press Secretary, the White House. 28 May 2011. *Fact Sheet: US-Poland Bilateral Defense Cooperation.*

[90] Davies, p. 30.

[91] Radiokrakow.pl. 12 June 2013. *Zaskakująca statystyka: Kraków się... wyludnia!*

[92] Wprost. 10 June 2013. *Agencje reklamowe walczą o billboardy.*

[93] Maciejasz, Dominika. Gazeta.pl. 11 June 2013. *Chcesz upiększyć miasto i posadzić rośliny? Grozi ci mandat.*

[94] Radłowska, Renata. Gazeta Kraków. 30 October 2013. *Pogotowie grafficiarskie.*

[95] TVN24.pl. 14 November 2013. *Kraków walczy z graffiti. "Część wandali zatrzymujemy na gorącym uczynku".*

[96] Krakow Post. 11 June 2013. *Krakow authorities take note of civic activism.*

[97] Kuraś, Bartłomiej. Gazeta Kraków. 25 November 2013. *Jest decyzja o zakazie palenia węglem. Kraków odetchnie.*

[98] Ibid., Brunnstrom. Also Waterfield, Bruno. The Telegraph. 3 May 2012. *Russia threatens NATO with military strikes over missile defence system.* Also Marcus, Jonathan. BBC News. 18 December 2013. *Missile deployment signals a more assertive Russia.*

[99] Applebaum, Chapter 6 and Davies, p. 72.

[100] Snyder, Chapters 11-14.

[101] The Economist. 10 March 2012. *Poland and Lithuania: bad blood.*

[102] Thenews.pl. 23 August 2011. *Polish nationalists vandalize Lithuanian signs.*

[103] TVN24.pl. 9 August 2013. *Antylitewskie hasła kibiców Lecha. MSZ potępia, PZPN przeprasza.*

[104] Newsweek Polska. 21 July 2011. *Przewodnicząca litewskiego Sejmu: Stosunki z Polską mają być strategiczne.* Also Stratfor Global Intelligence. 14 February 2013. *When Polish and Lithuanian interests align.*

[105] The Economist. 16 June 2005. *Bordering on madness.*

[106] Snyder, pp. 266-268.

[107] Marin, Anaïs. Ośrodek Studiów Wschodnich. 29 April 2013. *Trading off sovereignty. The outcome of Belarus's integration with Russia in the security and defense field.*

[108] Konończuk, Wojciech. Ośrodek Studiów Wschodnich. 27 November 2013. *Ukraine withdraws from signing the Association Agreement in Vilnius: The motives and implications.*

[109] Alsund, Anders. BBC News. 11 December 2013. *Ukraine crisis: Yanukovych and the tycoons.*

[110] Ćwiek, Joanna. Rzeczpospolita. 4 March 2013. *Polska skazana na imigrantów.*

[111] Bukowczyk, John. pp. 66-67.

Made in the USA
Middletown, DE
18 June 2015